Fight As Long As Possible: The Battle of Newport Barracks, North Carolina February 2, 1864

By

Eric A. Lindblade

Ten Roads Publishing

Gettysburg, Pennsylvania

Published by Ten Roads Publishing, LLC.

201 Chambersburg Street

Gettysburg, PA 17325

First Edition

ISBN 978-0-9825275-3-5

Cover image from *The Story of American Heroism: Thrilling Narratives of Personal Adventures during the Great Civil War, as told by the Medal Winners and Roll of Honor Men* published in 1897 by J.W. Jones, Springfield, Ohio

PRINTED AND BOUND IN THE UNITED STATES OF AMERICA

Contents

Introduction: i

Chapter One: 1
"I can now spare the troops..."

Chapter Two: 13
"All the assistance in your power..."

Chapter Three: 32
"This is a great country for a poor man to live in..."

Chapter Four: 49
"A very long and fatiguing but energetic march..."

Chapter Five: 58
"The Cavalry Dashed Furiously Forward..."

Chapter Six: 71
"A Spirited Resistance..."

Chapter Seven: 83
"Such a scurrying time you never saw..."

Chapter Eight: 96
"Fight As Long As Possible..."

Chapter Nine: 115
"One of the greatest panics..."

Epilogue: 134
The Cost and Legacy of the Battle of Newport Barracks, February 2, 1864

Appendix A: 148
Roster of Confederate and Union Casualties from February 2, 1864

Appendix B: 155
Medal of Honor Recipients at the Battle of Newport Barracks, February 2, 1864

To my parents, Eric and Susan Lindblade

and

To the men from Massachusetts, New York, North Carolina, South Carolina, Vermont and Virginia, who fought on February 2, 1864 in and around Newport Barracks, North Carolina

Introduction

History is like a vast puzzle for which most of the pieces will forever remain missing. It is the historian's mission to gather as many of the surviving pieces as he or she can, and from as many sources as possible (written, visual, oral, and physical). The historian must then evaluate all of these pieces, and develop a rational interpretation of the subject at hand- but always realizing that most of the pieces will forever remain missing, and that new and potentially significant evidence will continue to surface indefinitely.[1]

-William A. Frassanito

Ever since I was a child, I have been fascinated by the events and personalities associated with the American Civil War, especially those from my native state of North Carolina. In 1998, at the age of fifteen, I moved to Newport, North Carolina. Shortly after moving, I found a copy of a small book that ultimately led me on the journey that resulted in the writing of this book. That book was Newport, NC during the Civil War by William Pohresky. Written in 1978, Pohresky through his research located many of the

---

[1] William A. Frassanito. *Early Photography At Gettysburg* (Gettysburg, PA: Thomas Publications, 1995) x.

sites associated with the Newport and western Carteret County area during the Civil War. Not only did this book give me my first bit of information on what happened in Newport during the Civil War, but more importantly it described where they occurred.

With this information in hand, I would visit often the sites contained in the book, the entire time fascinated by the idea that I had a Civil War site, and even better a battlefield, almost in my backyard. Captivated by those early visits, I soon found myself wanting to learn as much as I could about the stories of the people and places associated with Newport during the Civil War, more specifically the Battle of Newport Barracks fought on February 2, 1864. From that point on I began to gather bits and pieces of information, with people often asking me questions about what happened. In 2006, after a number of people recommending that I do so, the writing of this book began.

From my earliest treks exploring the fields around Newport, I began to ask myself two basic, yet important, questions that have always guided my research on the Battle of Newport Barracks: How did the battle develop and unfold? And what was the experience of those individuals, military and civilian, who were caught up in that moment of history? As I delved further into my research I was able to uncover and discover some of those puzzle pieces, but also, much to my chagrin, discovered the inherent problems associated with historical research, as eloquently described by William A. Frassanito. To the best of my ability I have tried to put together the known pieces of the puzzle that is the Battle of Newport Barracks, all the while hoping my efforts might yet turn up other pieces helping to shed further light to what we already know.

One of the most glaring areas that posed a problem is the small number of Confederate primary sources relating to the battle, beyond the contemporary newspapers from 1864 and Official Reports, as compared to those found from Union participants. This is a problem many Civil War historians encounter, and is not specific to this work or the lack of effort by the author in attempting to locate such sources. While there are a few very good accounts, they unfortunately do not equal the number found from Union troops. I have used those

Confederate primary sources as much as I could in this book, but due to the number available have had to rely often on the same primary sources. I hope with the publication of this book that more Confederate sources will turn up, thus adding more in terms of depth and perspective to the Confederate experience in the battle.

While I am not the first historian to write on the subject of the Battle of Newport Barracks, I have benefited greatly from those works that have come before. Along with William Pohresky, Donald Wickman and Paul Zeller in the past five years have both written regimental histories of the 9th Vermont Volunteer Infantry that discussed the role played by the 9th Vermont in the fighting in and around Newport Barracks. For the most part the work of these historians would be the extent of any modern writing on the battle.

All three books are excellent, but each has drawbacks in terms of telling the story of the Battle of Newport Barracks. For the books by Wickman and Zeller, the focus of their work is the entire history of the 9th Vermont, which the battle of February 2, 1864 played but a part. This, by its very nature, precludes any full historical treatment of the battle, especially the part played by the Confederate adversaries of the 9th Vermont. In the case of Pohresky, his book on Newport and the Civil War gives an overview, but far from a detailed account, of the battle.

My goal for writing this book was to combine the research that has come before, with additional new research, to create a stand-alone book on the battle that places the fighting, along with the events that preceded and followed it, into not only the larger context of the Civil War in eastern North Carolina, but also the war as a whole.

A common view of the fighting on February 2, 1864 was that it was nothing more than a mere diversionary skirmish for the larger operations at New Bern, but this view does a disservice to what transpired and to the men who fought there. In terms of the numbers engaged the Battle of Newport Barracks was the largest battle fought during the Civil War in Carteret County, and in the grim arithmetic of men killed and wounded, the bloodiest. Along with the size and human cost, the Southern victory in the battle is one of the few occasions where Confederate forces in eastern North Carolina saw the fortunes of war smile on them, even if for just a few days.

In addition to telling the story of the Battle of Newport Barracks, I hope this book is a tribute to those who fought, sacrificed, and in some cases perished in the fighting that day. While not as well known, or as large, as battles such as Shiloh, Antietam, or Gettysburg; the fact remains that those who lost their lives in and around Newport Barracks, or later as a result of their wounds, sacrificed as much as those who fell in more famous locations such as the Hornet's Nest, the Bloody Lane, or Devil's Den with the loss of life no less tragic to the families of those soldiers.

Some men would bear the scars of that day for the rest of their lives, a painful reminder of February 2, 1864; others would emerge unharmed with the vivid images of the fighting seared into their consciousness. After the battle, the participants of the fight followed any number of paths. Some marched on and continued to serve until the end of our nation's bloodiest conflict; others would desert back to their homes and away from the hardships of army life.

Some would go on to be wounded or killed at a later battles in the war; while some would languish and die in prison camps deprived of any semblance of humane treatment.

When the war was finally over, some of the participants at Newport Barracks would become civic and community leaders of renown, some helped to form colleges and universities, and one soldier would gain an infamous reputation for the crime he was said to have committed in the form of a popular ballad. But in most cases the men who fought at Newport Barracks simply went home to start or, in some cases, rebuild their lives interrupted by war. No matter what their lives held for them, the soldiers on each side always had a permanent connection to the tiny eastern North Carolina village of Shepardsville, later to be named Newport.

As with any book, the final product is not simply the result of one person's efforts. Numerous individuals have played a part in what has become Fight As Long As Possible: The Battle of Newport Barracks, North Carolina, February 2, 1864.

First and foremost I would like to thank my parents, Eric and Susan Lindblade, for their love and support throughout my life and during the research and writing of this book. Unbeknownst to them at the time, on a trip to see family in Maine in 1989, they listened to a six-year voice from the backseat to visit the battlefield at Gettysburg, Pennsylvania and in doing so gave me my first exposure to a place that has had an indelible impact on my life. From that time on they took an active interest in my passion for the study of the Civil War and helped to foster it through countless books purchased and thousands of miles traveled taking me to visit Civil War sites as a child. My father, Eric Lindblade, provided the editing for the book, and offered invaluable advice during the writing process. I truly could not have better parents and my life is infinitely greater for having them in my life.

Outside my parents, the other great influence on me, and ultimately this book, was the teachers I was privileged and lucky enough to have in school throughout my educational process. It was my kindergarten teacher, Ms. Carolyn Quick who first taught me about the Civil War and as a result ignited a spark and a passion for history that continues to this day. I would also like to take this opportunity to thank Ms. Laura Swink, Ms. Evelyn Faison, Mr. Dennis Carter, Mr. O.J. West, Mr. Garland Whitaker, Mr. Colin Mayo, and Mr. Benjy Downing. I owe them all a debt I can never repay and in a small way I hope this book is a testament to their impact and influence, not just on me, but to countless students through the years.

I would like to thank my long time friends from North Carolina, Morgan Barbour, Brandon Blackman, Joey Greene, Leah Knox and John Moore for their encouragement and friendship for as long as I have known them and during the writing of this book. I could not ask for better friends.

Since moving to Gettysburg in August of 2008 numerous individuals have played a role that ultimately led to the publication of this book. First, I would like to thank my friend and business partner at Ten Roads Publishing Jim Glessner for his support and assistance throughout this process. Michael Waricher and Karl Stelly reviewed sections of the manuscript and encouragement throughout. I would also like to thank Erik Dorr for, in addition to reviewing the manuscript, helping me to acquire the flag that was carried by the 9th Vermont Infantry at the Battle of Newport Barracks, and for allowing it to be on display at his Gettysburg Museum of History, preserving for future generations a tangible connection to the fighting that day.

Living in Gettysburg has allowed me to opportunity to meet a number of talented historians who have helped to make me not only a better writer, but also a better historian. Even since I first read his Gettysburg: A Journey in Time in the sixth grade I have been influenced by the works of William A. Frassanito. I have had the privilege to have numerous conversations with Bill and I am a better historian because of them.

Timothy H. Smith, through his role as Research Historian at the Adams County Historical Society, was very helpful in his discovery of two soldiers wounded at Newport Barracks in the Medical and Surgical History of the Civil War. Historians John Archer, James Hessler, and John Hoptak have been the sources of invaluable advice during the research and writing process. I am grateful to all for their advice and I am glad to call them friends.

I first met Michael Vice, former curator at the Gettysburg National Military Park, when I was in the fourth grade and later he was the first sergeant when I began reenacting in 1997 with F Company of the 21st Virginia. Through visits to Gettysburg and in the field reenacting, Mike has had a lasting influence on me as a historian and for that I thank him.

Paul Branch at Fort Macon State Park was very helpful in the early stages of my research and answered many of the questions I had about the battle.

Last but certainly I would like to thank the staffs at a number of libraries and repositories who aided in the research process, their time and effort has not been forgotten and is greatly appreciated.

In North Carolina: The History Place in Morehead City, The North Carolina Collection and the Special Collections Department at the Joyner Library at East Carolina University in Greenville, The William Perkins Library at Duke University in Durham, The Southern Historical Collection at the Wilson Library at the University of North Carolina in Chapel Hill, The North Carolina State Archives in Raleigh, The Kellenberger Research Room at the New Bern-Craven

County Library in New Bern, and the Davidson County Historical Society in Lexington.

In Pennsylvania: The Gettysburg National Military Park in Gettysburg, the Adams County Historical Society in Gettysburg, and The United States Army Heritage and Education Center in Carlisle.

And finally, The National Archives in Washington, D.C.

To anyone who assisted me that I have left out, my sincerest apologies and any errors in this book rest not with those who assisted me, but solely with the author.

Eric A. Lindblade
Gettysburg, Pennsylvania
June, 2010

In order to help orient the reader to the distances between the various locations in the book, this page has been provided. All of the locations are in terms of the 1864 distance, based on the road network of the era. For example, the modern distance between the town of Newport and Morehead City is around four miles; in 1864 it was closer to ten miles, as Morehead City was located farther east than it is today.

The following are the distances from Newport Barracks to the various locations:

Beaufort:	*15 miles*
Bogue Sound Blockhouse:	*4 miles*
Canady's Mills:	*5 miles*
Carolina City:	*8 miles*
Cedar Point:	*15 miles*
Gales Creek Blockhouse:	*5 miles*
Peletier's Mills:	*14 miles*
Morehead City:	*10 miles*
New Bern:	*25 miles*
Wilmington:	*75 miles*

Chapter One

"I can now spare the troops..."

"The time is at hand when, if an attempt can be made to capture the enemy's forces at New Berne, it should be done. I can now spare troops for the purpose, which will not be the case as spring approaches." So began General Robert E. Lee, commander of the Army of Northern Virginia, in a January 2, 1864 letter addressed to Confederate President Jefferson Davis; its contents outlined his recommendation for a campaign against the Union forces located in New Bern, North Carolina. Lee described the garrison at New Bern as being "so long unmolested, and experiences such a feeling of security, that it is represented as careless." In closing Lee stated that "a large amount of provisions and other supplies are said to be at New Berne, which are much wanted for this army, besides much that is reported in the country that will thus be made accessible to us.[1]" This letter set in motion the events that ultimately led to the Battle of Newport Barracks, fought exactly one month later on February 2, 1864.

As Lee and Davis were well aware, the supply routes in eastern North Carolina, especially the Wilmington and Weldon Railroad, were critical to military operations in Virginia and elsewhere; as a result the prospect of Union incursions against them were a constant cause for worry by Confederate leadership. New Bern, with its location, was well suited to being a base of operations for such efforts by Union troops into the coastal plain of North Carolina and beyond.

Since the Union occupation of the region in 1862, a number of raids by Union forces had proved just how tenuous the supply lines in eastern North Carolina were without adequate defenses. In December of 1862, Union troops under the command

[1] *Official Records of the War of the Rebellion: Series 1 Volume 32*. 1061 (This series and volume are hereafter cited as *Official Records,* unless otherwise noted.)

of Major General John Foster made a demonstration against Goldsboro, and in the process ransacked the town of Kinston after dispatching the Confederate defenders.[2]

A few months later, in July of 1863, a force of Union cavalry under the command of Brigadier General Edward Potter moved against and raided key logistical targets throughout eastern North Carolina, including Greenville, Tarboro, and Rocky Mount.[3] In the same month, a surprise raid by a Union cavalry detachment under the command of Colonel Samuel P. Spear threatened the railroad bridge located at Weldon, a key point on the Wilmington and Weldon line.[4] Just three days before Lee outlined his recommendation for an offensive operation against New Bern to Davis, a sharp skirmish took place near

---

[2] John Barrett. *The Civil War in North Carolina* (Chapel Hill, North Carolina: University of North Carolina Press, 1963) 144. (Hereafter cited as *Barrett*)

[3] Ibid. 164. The 23rd New York Cavalry was part of the force that took part in the raid. They would later see action at Newport Barracks on February 2, 1864.

[4] Ibid.

Greenville between Union and Confederate cavalry on December 30, 1863.[5]

The results of these raids were not just in the damage to the logistical abilities of Confederates in the area, but in the deployment of thousands of troops needed to defend the lines of supply. If Confederate troops were successful in reclaiming parts of eastern North Carolina it would force a drastic change in Union strategy for the upcoming year, along with giving Lee and the Army of Northern Virginia a clear line of supply from Wilmington, North Carolina all the way to Petersburg, Virginia without the threat of raid or capture, along with freeing up thousands of needed troops for the front lines in Virginia.

Another pressing matter on the minds of Confederate leaders was the blockade of the southern coastline that included North Carolina. Since 1861 the Union Navy had been tasked with blockading operations, whose objective was to cut off the supplies and commerce going in and out of southern ports. By

---

5 D.H. Hill Jr. *Confederate Military History: Volume IV North Carolina* (Atlanta, Georgia: Confederate Publishing Company, 1899) 218.

1864 many ports throughout the South had fallen under Union control, further complicating matters of supply for the Confederacy.

The approaches to Wilmington, North Carolina and the port located there were guarded by a strong line of coastal fortifications, most importantly Fort Fisher, whose long range artillery kept the Union blockaders at bay. Through Wilmington much needed goods for the Confederate war effort still continued to flow and if Union forces could capture the city it would be a disastrous setback to the Confederacy. Since falling into Union hands in April of 1862 the port at Beaufort, North Carolina had proven to be an important refueling and resupply point for the North Atlantic Blockading Squadron and any attempt against Wilmington would undoubtedly use Beaufort as a logistical base. If the Union lost the use of Beaufort it would force the blockading fleet, or an attacking force against Wilmington, to use the supply depots at Norfolk and Hampton Roads, Virginia thus reducing the amount of time ships could be effective in operation off the North Carolina coast.

Along with the military gains that could be made, there were clear political implications to such a

Confederate offensive in eastern North Carolina. John W. Moore would write after the war that conditions in eastern North Carolina in 1864 "grew hourly more deplorable.[6]" Moore would continue:

> Frequent incursions of the enemy resulted in the destruction of property of all kinds. Especially were horses and mules objects of plunder. Pianos and other costly furniture were seized and sent North, while whole regiments of "bummers" wantonly defaced and ruined the fairest homesteads in eager search for hidden treasure. The "Buffaloes," in gangs of a dozen men, infested the swamps and made night hideous with their horrid visitations.[7]

Buffaloes were gangs of Union "bushwhackers" who operated in gangs of around a dozen based often in the swamps in eastern North Carolina; emerging at night to "visit their former neighbors, especially those who sympathized with the South, and to perpetrate

---

[6] John W. Moore. *History of North Carolina; From the Earliest Discoveries to the Present Time, Volume II* (Raleigh, North Carolina: Alfred Williams & Co., Publishers, 1880) 251. (Hereafter cited as *Moore*). John W. Moore was the commander of the 3rd North Carolina Battalion of Light Artillery. It would be Company A from the 3rd Battalion that would form part of the Confederate artillery at the Battle of Newport Barracks.

[7] Ibid.

every type of violence and crime.[8]" President Jefferson Davis realized a series of military successes in the region would have positive effect on the morale of North Carolina citizens, along with reducing the pillaging and plundering taking place. Politically, in a state that was vital to the Confederate war effort in terms of men and material, such success would effectively undermine the small, but vocal, peace movement in the state. On January 20, 1864 General Lee would write that military successes in eastern North Carolina will have "the happiest effect in North Carolina and inspire the people.[9]"

The plan of operations against New Bern, approved by President Jefferson Davis, was designed in large part by Brigadier General Robert F. Hoke, a native North Carolinian and rising star in the Army of Northern Virginia, who developed a "carefully prepared" plan for the capture of New Bern, which

---

8 *Barrett*, 174.

9 *Official Records, 1102.*

was "approved most heartily and authorized" by Lee.[10] Davis would write to Lee on January 4, 1864 to approve his recommendation and plan for the recapture of New Bern:

> Your suggestion is approved, but who can and will execute it? You could give it form, which would insure success, but without your personal attention I fear such failure as have elsewhere been suffered. It would be well to send the brigade, and if circumstances permit, you had better go down; otherwise I will go myself, though it could only be for a very few days, Congress being in session.[11]

The suggestion by Davis that Lee accompany the operation was a clear indication of the importance placed on the upcoming campaign, Davis going so far as to personally offer that he travel to North Carolina to oversee and command if necessary. Lee would decline the suggestion in his January 20 letter to Davis stating that "in view of the opinion expressed in your letter, I would go to North Carolina myself, but I

---

[10] Daniel W. Barefoot. *General Robert F. Hoke, Lee's Modest Warrior* (Winston- Salem, North Carolina: John F. Blair, Publisher, 2001) 107. (Hereafter cited as *Barefoot*)

[11] *Official Records, 1064.*

consider my presence here always necessary, especially now, when there is such a struggle to keep the army fed and clothed" but would later write "I will, however go to North Carolina if you think it is necessary.[12]" Lee would in turn recommend Robert Hoke for command of the operation, but Davis felt that Hoke, as a brigadier general, was not of sufficient rank to command such an important assignment and instead command was given to Major General George E. Pickett, of Gettysburg fame, instead.[13]

Since Hoke was the primary architect of the plan to recapture New Bern, he and his brigade of North Carolinians would join Pickett in the campaign, with Hoke acting as second in command. Pickett would command around thirteen thousand infantrymen from the brigades of Hoke, Seth Barton, Montgomery Corse, Thomas Clingman, Matt Ransom, and James Kemper, as well as artillery under the command of Major James Dearing, who was given the temporary rank of colonel for the operation.[14] A

---

[12] Ibid. 1101.

[13] *Barrett*, 203.

[14] *Official Records*, 1102.

handpicked detachment of Confederate sailors and marines, under the command of Commander John Taylor Wood, would join in the offensive. Wood was a trusted advisor to Jefferson Davis, along with being the nephew of the Confederate president.[15]

Pickett would take the troops under his command to Petersburg, Virginia and from there board trains for Goldsboro and finally on to Kinston, which was to be the staging area for the attack on New Bern. With the infantry under Pickett advancing on the city from three different directions, Wood with his sailors and marines would descend the Neuse River in launches to surprise and capture the gunboats located in the river, turning the guns on the Union troops in order to support the infantry attack.[16]

Along with the troops under Pickett, Lee requested that Major General W.H.C. Whiting, commander of the forces around Wilmington in the Department of the Cape Fear, assist in the operations. Lee wrote to Whiting on January 20:

---

[15] *Barefoot*, 108.

[16] *Official Records,* 1102.

An attack on New Berne is contemplated by the forces under the command of General Pickett. The time will be between the 25th and 28th instant. I request that you will give all the assistance in your power, especially by threatening simultaneously with your troops north of the Cape Fear the enemy's positions at Morehead City, and &c.[sic], so as to prevent their re-enforcing New Berne. General Pickett will telegraph you the day, by which you will know what is meant. Commit nothing to the telegraph on the subject, and keep the matter secret.[17]

The same day Lee would write to Pickett, then at Petersburg, giving further instructions on how to coordinate with Whiting. Lee would counsel Pickett on how to explain the sudden appearance of thirteen thousand Confederate infantry at Kinston:

When the day of attack is fixed notify General Whiting. If you have to use the telegraph, merely say, "The day is" – name the day of the month; he will comprehend. Commit nothing to the telegraph that may disclose your purpose. You must deceive the enemy as to your purpose, and conceal it from the citizens. As regards the concentration of troops, you may put it on the ground of apprehension of an attack from New Berne. General

[17] Ibid. 1103.

Hoke will give out that he is going to arrest deserters and recruit his diminished regiments.[18]

The need for absolute secrecy was critical to keeping the element of surprise on the side of the Confederates, without it Union reinforcements would pour into New Bern, increasing the difficulty in the capture of the city. The silence on the telegraph and the deliberate misinformation were further efforts to reduce the possibility of Union commanders in the area from being made aware as to the real plans that Pickett and his command had in store. Whiting would agree to assist Pickett, as requested by Lee, and it would be around two thousand soldiers from his command at Wilmington and Kenansville that would be tasked with cutting the key Union supply line from Beaufort to New Bern and ultimately would form the Confederate forces engaged in battle at Newport Barracks on February 2, 1864.

---

[18] Ibid.

Chapter Two

"All the assistance in your power..."

Major General W.H.C. Whiting, in compliance with the request of General Robert E. Lee to "give all the assistance in your power" in support of the offensive at New Bern, selected Brigadier General James Martin to command the Confederate forces that would threaten "the enemy's positions at Morehead City, and &c [sic].[1]" By giving command to Martin, Whiting chose a highly capable and dependable officer with a proven record of experience. In the upcoming movements against Newport Barracks, Martin would once again prove his abilities as an officer.

James Green Martin was born in Elizabeth City, North Carolina on February 14, 1819, where he was named after his grandfather, a Methodist minister in Norfolk, Virginia. Martin was educated in Raleigh,

---

[1] *Official Records*, 1103.

North Carolina, and later would enter the United States Military Academy at West Point in 1836. He would graduate in 1840 ranked fourteenth in a class that included future Civil War generals Richard S. Ewell and George H. Thomas.[2] Martin fought with distinction during the Mexican War, where at the Battle of Churubusco he was wounded severely in the right arm resulting in its amputation.[3] For his gallant service in Mexico, Martin was brevetted major, and would continue to serve in the Army until the outbreak of war in 1861.

When North Carolina seceded from the Union on May 20, 1861, Martin resigned his commission in the United States Army. In large part because of his experience and reputation in the "old army," Martin was appointed on September 20 as the adjutant general of ten North Carolina regiments currently being raised in the state. Just a few days later he was

---

[2] William S. Powell, editor. *Dictionary of North Carolina Biography,* Volume *L-O.* (Chapel Hill and London: University of North Carolina Press, 1991) 226. (Hereafter cited as *Powell*)

[3] Ezra J. Warner. *Generals in Gray, Lives of the Confederate Commanders.* (Baton Rouge and London: Louisiana State University Press, 1959) 213. (Hereafter cited as *Warner*)

promoted, this time to adjutant general of all the military forces in the State of North Carolina. Martin was placed in charge of the organizing, arming, training, feeding, and clothing of North Carolina troops, as well as overseeing the defenses in the state.[4] His service in the provisioning of state troops was brilliantly successful, and resulted not only in North Carolina supplying more troops to Confederate armies than any other state, but also in being one of the best equipped.[5]

After the service rendered to his home state, Martin applied for a field command, and soon was appointed a brigadier general in the Confederate army.[6] In 1863, he was placed in command of an infantry brigade consisting of the 17th, 42nd, 50th, and 66th North Carolina regiments. Martin was a strict disciplinarian and the troops under him held the reputation as being a well-drilled and efficient group of soldiers. Despite his nature as a commander, the

---

4 *Powell*, 227.

5 *Warner*, 213-214.

6 Ibid.

troops under his command held him in high regard, affectionately referring to him as "Old One Wing," an allusion to the loss of his right arm in Mexico.[7]

The bulk of the force Martin would lead into battle at Newport Barracks consisted of two regiments of infantry from his brigade, the 17th and 42nd North Carolina. Both regiments spent the majority of their service, up to 1864, in North Carolina and while not as battle tested as other North Carolina regiments, they had some experience under fire, were well drilled, and led by competent officers. The men of the 17th and 42nd North Carolina, as was to be expected, were anxious for the chance to strike back against the Union occupiers of their home state and were more than ready to do their duty.

The 17th North Carolina of Martin's Brigade was the second incarnation of an infantry regiment to bear that numerical designation, and many from the original regiment would fill the ranks in the reorganized version. It would be composed of men from Martin, Hyde, Bertie, Hertford, Washington,

---

7 *Powell*, 227.

Edgecombe, Pitt, Perquimans, and Tyrell counties from the eastern section of the state, along with Person and Granville counties from the Piedmont. The first organization of the 17th North Carolina had been captured on August 27, 1861 at Hatteras Island by Union forces.

Two companies of the regiment would escape capture that day, only to be captured themselves at Fort Bartow on Roanoke Island [8] After becoming prisoners of war and being exchanged, the 17th North Carolina was reorganized at Camp Mangum, near Raleigh, North Carolina, in May of 1862 and mustered into service for three years or the duration of the war.[9] Wilson Lamb, a lieutenant in Company F of the 17th North Carolina, would describe the service of the regiment in 1862 and 1863 as follows:

---

[8] Walter Clark, editor. *Histories of the Several Regiments and Battalions from North Carolina in the Great War 1861-1865.* Volume II. (Hereafter cited as *Clark Volume II*) 3.

[9] Weymouth T. Jordan, Jr. *North Carolina Troops 1861-1865: A Roster, Volume VI Infantry.* (Raleigh: North Carolina Office of Archives and History, Third Printing 2004) 201. (Hereafter cited as *17th Roster*)

The Seventeenth was assigned to service in Eastern North Carolina and performed picket duty watching the enemy at New Bern, Washington, and Plymouth. In December, 1862, a detachment from the regiment with a squadron of cavalry from Colonel Evans' regiment (Sixty-third North Carolina) and Moore's Battery, all under Lieutenant-Colonel Lamb, captured Plymouth. Another detachment drove the enemy from Washington, N.C. Many minor raids and surprises of the enemy's outposts cleverly managed by Captain William Biggs, Lieutenants Hardison, Grimes, Cotton, and others gave indication of what might be expected of the regiment when it should have the opportunity of displaying its fighting qualities.

In 1863 the regiment was brigaded with the Forty-second, Fiftieth, and Sixty-sixth Regiments and placed under the command of Brigadier-General James G. Martin, and stationed at Fort Branch, Kinston, and Wilmington, and was thoroughly drilled and disciplined by that splendid organizer and disciplinarian.[10]

To many in the 17th North Carolina the duty in eastern North Carolina was an enjoyable experience because of the close proximity to their homes and families. W.H. Wyatt, a private from Company H, recounted after the war, that it was not uncommon to see soldiers absent during roll call, with most of the

---

[10] *Clark Volume II,* 2-3.

absent living nearby. These soldiers frequently "ran the blockade" after roll call and would go home "for clean clothing or supplies of food, tobacco, etc.[11]" Wyatt would later recount the feelings of many in the ranks when they were ordered to move from the camps close to home to a new location:

> So many of our men lived within reach of the camp and got clean clothes and good things to eat from home every week, that we were unusually clean and sleek in appearance, and came to be called the "band-box regiment," and others were jealous of us. So it came to pass that one day we were informed that we were to go to the front, and that another regiment was to take our place. The news caused much surprise and regret in camp; surprise, grief, and tears in the homes of those who resided within visiting distance of the camp.[12]

On November 9, 1863 the 17th North Carolina arrived in Wilmington where it joined the other regiments making up Martin's Brigade; barely a

---

[11] W.H. Wyatt. *Around The Camp Fire: Remembered Incidents and People of the Civil War*. Francis M. Manning Papers, Collection Number 488, East Carolina University Manuscript Collection, J.Y. Joyner Library, East Carolina University, Greenville, North Carolina. (Cited hereafter as *Wyatt*)

[12] Ibid.

month later four companies would be sent to Kenansville for winter quarters. The 17th North Carolina was under the command of twenty-eight year old Lieutenant Colonel John Calhoun Lamb, an unmarried merchant from Martin County.[13] Soon Lamb and the so called "band-box regiment" would have the opportunity to display their fighting qualities.

While the first organization of the 17th North Carolina were becoming prisoners of war, the men who later formed the first four companies of the 42nd North Carolina were part of the guard detail at the military prison in Salisbury, North Carolina. These men were part of Major George Gibbs' Prison Guard Battalion and would form companies A, B, C, and D of the newly organized 42nd North Carolina. In addition, six newly raised companies were added to reach the full complement of ten companies for the regiment in April of 1862. Major Gibbs would be appointed

---

[13] Robert K. Krick. *Lee's Colonels: A Biographical Register of the Field Officers of the Army of Northern Virginia, Fifth Edition, Revised*(Wilmington: Broadfoot Publishing Company, 2009) 229. (Hereafter cited as *Krick*)

colonel and the regiment attended camp of instruction at Camp Fisher near Salisbury. During this time companies from the 42nd North Carolina were detailed as guards at the Salisbury prison.[14]

The 42nd North Carolina would have the benefit of an experienced group of officers leading the new regiment. Major Thomas J. Brown would write after the war that "many of the officers of the Forty-second Regiment had entered the Civil War at its beginning, so that they were well versed in military science at the time of the organization of the regiment." Brown would continue: "The Forty-second was a splendid aggregation of men, composed of many of the best men of Mecklenburg, Catawba, Iredell, Rowan, Davie, Davidson, and Stanly counties. The personnel was

---

[14] Weymouth T. Jordan, Jr. *North Carolina Troops 1861-1865: A Roster, Volume X Infantry.* (Raleigh: North Carolina Office of Archives and History, Second Printing 2004) 201. (Hereafter cited as *42nd Roster*) 187. Gibbs resigned command on January 7, 1864 and later served at the Andersonville prison. During the trial for war crimes of Henry Wirz, commander of Andersonville, Gibbs would be subpoenaed to appear in the trial.

excellent and the troops were well equipped."[15] In addition men from Union and Wilkes counties served in the regiment.

In the summer of 1862 the regiment was moved by rail to Richmond and finally on to Lynchburg, Virginia. Once again they were detailed to guard Union prisoners of war, this time prisoners captured by Thomas J. "Stonewall" Jackson during his campaign in the Shenandoah Valley.[16] The 42nd North Carolina would return to North Carolina in January of 1863, where it went into winter quarters near Garysburg.[17] On March 23, 1863 a special battalion of the 42nd North Carolina, consisting of companies B, E, and F, under the command of Lieutenant Colonel John E. Brown attacked and routed a camp of "Buffaloes" near Wingfield, North Carolina.[18] After destroying the camp, Brown and a number of the soldiers under his command were trapped on the east bank of the Chowan River by Union gunboats, forced

---

15 Ibid. 792.

16 *42nd Roster*, 187.

17 *Clark Volume II*, 793.

18 *42nd Roster*, 187.

to fight off a superior force of cavalry and United States Marines the next day.[19] The fight that ensued was described as follows:

> Upon learning that the marines had landed, and were coming up to the row boats, Colonel Brown planned an ambuscade. But the surprise was for the Confederates, who were fired upon before they knew the whereabouts of the enemy. Colonel Brown formed his men on one side of an old field not more than 150 yards from the Federal troops, who were concealed in the woods on the other side of the field. The Confederate advance was as cool as if on dress-parade. The Federals held their fire until the Confederates were within 60 to 70 yards and then fired a volley. Fortunately, their fire was too high and a storm of bullets sped over the heads of the Confederates. A charge was made, with the "Rebel Yell," which struck terror into the hearts of the Federals, and they fell back to the swamp. Here Lieutenant W.C. Willson and Private E. Collett were wounded, apparently mortally. Both, however, recovered from their wounds. Lieutenant Wilson became a minister of the Gospel and still survives. It was learned afterwards that sixteen Federals were killed in this fight. Here for the first time the men charged with the "Rebel Yell," and one Federal marine swore that there must have been 500 Confederates charging, as no fifty men could make such an awful noise.

---

[19] Ibid.

> A relief expedition was formed by the men on the other shore of the river, and Colonel Brown and his men were brought out in safety by midnight.[20]

In December of 1863 the 42nd North Carolina settled into winter quarters at Camp Burgywn, near Wilmington, joining the other regiments of Martin's Brigade.[21] On January 4, 1864, Colonel George Gibbs would resign as commander of the 42nd North Carolina; Lieutenant Colonel John Edmunds Brown was immediately promoted to colonel and placed in command of the regiment. Brown was thirty-three years old and hailed from Mecklenburg County, where before the war he was an attorney. His wife, Laura Morrison Brown, was the sister of the wife of Thomas J. "Stonewall" Jackson.[22] While at Camp Burgywn, the 42nd North Carolina continued to drill through the winter months:

> They were under the most rigid discipline, and were systematically drilled in all the maneuvers of military tactics.

[20] *Clark Volume II*, 794-795.

[21] 42nd *Roster*, 188.

[22] *Krick, 68.*

General Martin was a West Pointer and was noted for the great efficiency and rapid movement of his troops in brigade drill.[23]

While the men in the ranks, it would be assumed, were not fond of the constant drill, Colonel Brown must have been pleased, as it was said that "Colonel Brown would rather drill than eat.[24]" In less than a month, the lessons of the parade ground and drill field would be put to the test.

Joining the operation with Martin, in support of the infantry, would be artillery composed of Company A of the 3rd Battalion North Carolina Light Artillery and the Staunton Hill Artillery from Virginia. In addition, two companies of cavalry, Company E of the 5th North Carolina and Company K of the 5th South Carolina, accompanied the infantry and artillery. In the upcoming fighting at Newport Barracks, these soldiers would provide valuable and effective service in the field.

---

23 *Clark Volume II*, 796.

24 Idid. 792.

Company A of the 3rd Battalion North Carolina Light Artillery was recruited from Northampton County, North Carolina and fittingly Company A was referred to as the "Northampton Artillery."[25] In command of the "Northampton Artillery" was twenty-nine year old Captain Andrew Jackson Ellis. Ellis attended the University of North Carolina, but eventually enrolled at the University of Pennsylvania in Philadelphia, where he earned a degree in medicine. Dr. Ellis soon returned to Garysburg and established his medical practice in the area. Despite his educational achievements, when Ellis was appointed to command Company A he had no prior military training or experience.[26]

The 3rd Battalion briefly served with the Army of Northern Virginia in the fall of 1862, but was never engaged. In addition to this service, they defended the critical Richmond, Fredericksburg, and Potomac Railroad Bridge over the North Anna River during the

---

[25] H. James Keith. *3rd Battalion North Carolina Light Artillery: "Moore's Battalion," C.S.A.* (Morrisville: Lulu Enterprises, 2007) 15. (Hereafter cited as *Keith*)

[26] Ibid. 19.

Fredericksburg Campaign in December of 1862.[27] In November of 1863, Major John W. Moore, commander of the 3rd Battalion, was assigned to the command of troops at Kenansville and would bring Company A with him, while the remainder of the battalion stayed in the Wilmington area. Ellis and his gunners would be armed with three six-pound guns and a three-inch ordinance rifle and would use them to great effect at Newport Barracks.[28]

Along with the 3rd Battalion North Carolina Light Artillery was the Staunton Hill Artillery organized in Charlotte County, Virginia in September of 1861. Captain Charles Bruce, a thirty-five year old Harvard-educated planter and member of the Virginia State Senate, recruited and equipped the battery out of his own pocket. It was estimated that Bruce's personal wealth was worth close to one million dollars

---

[27] Louis H. Manarin. *North Carolina Troops 1861-1865: A Roster, Volume I Artillery*. (Raleigh: North Carolina Office of Archives and History, Third Printing 2004) 335.

[28] *Keith, 75.*

in 1861. The battery was named after Staunton Hill, the large estate owned by Bruce in Charlotte County.[29]

Unlike most Virginia artillery units, the Staunton Hill Artillery did not see service in its home state, and instead was sent to Savannah, Georgia and finally to Wilmington. In May of 1862, Captain Bruce resigned his command on account of his health and to return to politics, along with his state senate seat. First Lieutenant Andrew J. Paris was promoted to captain and assumed command of the battery.[30] Captain Paris and his battery would be armed with four twelve-pounder Dahlgren guns and two twelve-pound howitzers.[31]

Company K of the 5th South Carolina Cavalry was mustered into Confederate service in Columbia, South Carolina on December 30, 1862. Originally known as the "Mountain Rangers," the men raised for

---

[29] Jeffrey C. Weaver. *Branch, Harrington, and Staunton Hill Artillery: The Virginia Regimental Histories Series.* (Lynchburg: H.E. Howard Inc., 1997) 82.

[30] Ibid. 85.

[31] Ibid. 93.

the company hailed mainly from the Spartanburg, Union, and York Districts, with some men calling the Newberry and Laurens Districts home. Their commander, Captain Joseph Gist Harlan, a planter and mechanic from Unionville, South Carolina, was forty-two at the time of the Battle of Newport Barracks.[32]

Gist had previously seen experience as the First Sergeant in Company D of the famed Hampton Legion. In July of 1863, the men of Company K were transferred from their posts around Charleston, South Carolina to the post of Kenansville, North Carolina, before being moved once again to Wilmington in November of 1863. It would be in Wilmington where the South Carolinians were attached to James Martin's Confederate command for the operations against Newport Barracks.[33]

Joining their fellow cavalrymen from South Carolina was Company E of the 5th North Carolina

---

[32] York County in the Civil War, *http://freepages.genealogy.rootsweb.com/~york/_indexYorkCivilWar.htm*

[33] Ibid.

Cavalry. The men of Company E of the 5th North Carolina Cavalry, known as the "Vance Troop," were mustered into service in 1862 and hailed primarily from Chatham County, but would later see an influx of men enlisting from Onslow County. Company E was under the command of Captain Thomas W. Harris.[34]

The first part of their service saw Company E, with the rest of the 5th North Carolina Cavalry, operating in eastern North Carolina. On December 16, 1862, the 5th would come under artillery fire at the Battle of White Hall, near Kinston, but remained in reserve.[35] In May of 1863, Company E was stationed at Huggins Farm in Onslow County, while the rest of their regiment was ordered the join the cavalry of the Army of Northern Virginia under the command of Major General J.E.B. Stuart. In November of 1863 they were ordered to move to Kenansville, and the company would remain there until taking part in the Battle of Newport Barracks.

---

[34] Louis H. Manarin. *North Carolina Troops 1861-1865: A Roster, Volume II Cavalry*. (Raleigh, North Carolina: North Carolina Office of Archives and History, Third Printing 2004) 405.

[35] Ibid. 367.

Unbeknownst to Union forces in and around Newport Barracks, near the small village of Sheppardsville in Carteret County, North Carolina, Martin and his nearly 2,000 troops, composed of infantry, artillery, and cavalry, would soon be heading on a collision course towards them.

Chapter Three

"This is a great country for a poor man to live in..."

In February of 1864, the village of Shepardsville, North Carolina, now current-day Newport, consisted of around fifteen homes, four stores, and a church. The small town was located on the north bank of the Newport River.[1] Shepardsville had little military value to either side, but the railroad trestle over the Newport River was an important segment of the Union supply lines in the region. It was over this trestle that the Atlantic and North Carolina Railroad, with its terminus in Morehead City, crossed heading west towards New Bern. The railroad provided an efficient means to transport supplies and troops between the coast and New Bern,

---

[1] W.L Pohresky. *Newport, NC during the Civil War* (Havelock, NC: The Print Shop, 1978) 4-5. (Hereafter cited as *Pohresky*). Union and Confederate soldiers used different names for Newport during the Civil War. Union soldiers tended to refer to village near the barracks as Newport, while Confederates referred to it as Shepardsville. In 1866, the General Assembly of North Carolina would charter the town as Newport. The use of Newport to describe the area dates back to the early 1700s.

along with other Union controlled areas. Aware of the importance of the Newport River crossing, Union commanders moved quickly to fortify and protect the railroad trestle.

The first soldiers to be stationed in the Newport area during the war were a company of Confederates from the 7th North Carolina Infantry who were quartered in log barracks north of town during the winter of 1861. When Union troops under Major General Ambrose Burnside moved into the area in March of 1862, the 5th Rhode Island would move into the barracks abandoned by the Confederates. Within two weeks the 5th Rhode Island was replaced by the 9th New Jersey, who began construction of new barracks and earthworks south of the Newport River defending the railroad trestle.[2] The 9th New Jersey, in addition to the barracks south of town, constructed the fortifications at Canady's Mill and the blockhouses located at Bogue Sound and Gales Creek. The fortifications around Newport Barracks were built of earth about twelve feet tall, in addition abatises were constructed.[3] At the time of the battle in February of

---

[2] *Pohresky*, 5.

[3] Ibid. 7.

1864, the garrison at Newport Barracks consisted of the 9th Vermont Infantry, the 23rd New York Cavalry, and Company D of the 2nd Massachusetts Heavy Artillery.

In the spring of 1862, the growing demand for troops in the field prompted President Abraham Lincoln to issue a call for 300,000 additional men to help put down the rebellion, with each state expected to meet its prescribed quota to comply with the order. In Vermont Governor Frederick Holbrook moved quickly to raise the three regiments of infantry that were requested of his state. The men formed the 9th Vermont were recruited that summer throughout the state, with recruiting stations set up in Bennington, Bradford, Brattleboro, Burlington, Hyde Park, Irasburgh, Middlebury, Perkinsville, Plainfield, Rutland, St. Johnsbury, and Swanton. Six weeks after the call from Lincoln had been received; the 9th Vermont was in camp and a short time later sent to the field under the command of Colonel George J. Stannard.[4] The 9th Vermont had the distinction of

[4] George Benedict. *Vermont in the Civil War, Volume II* (Burlington, VT: Free Press Association, 1888) 183. (Hereafter cited as *Benedict*) George J. Stannard, the first colonel of the 9th

being one of the very first regiments to be organized and mustered into service after the order for the additional 300,000 soldiers.

On July 16th, 1862, the 9th Vermont was the first regiment to march through New York City after Lincoln's call for troops. A large number of citizens welcomed the regiment at their camp near Madison Square and lined the streets of the city to watch as the 9th Vermont passed through. The July 17, 1862 issue of the *New York Tribune* described the scene in detail:

> The Green Mountain boys are the first to respond to the call of the president for additional troops. The march of this magnificent body of 1000 men through the aristocratic avenues and the grand thoroughfares of trade and traffic excited unusual interest and provoked the most enthusiastic demonstrations. The doors, windows, and balconies of the brown stone palaces were graced with fashion, wealth, and beauty, and Broadway was lined with vast multitudes of men and women eager to honor the Green Mountain boys as they marched to the music of the Union.[5]

Vermont, would go on to famously command a brigade of Vermont troops at Gettysburg, who helped to repulse Pickett's Charge on July 3, 1863.

[5] *Benedict*, 185.

Soon the pomp and parade atmosphere was replaced by the serious work of military service. The 9th Vermont was ordered to Winchester, Virginia in July of 1862, much to the disappointment of many in the ranks who hoped to be attached to the famous First Vermont Brigade, then serving in the Army of the Potomac. While at Winchester the regiment performed camp duties and constructed a bastioned fort known as Fort Sigel. The monotony and difficulty of camp duty, away from the active front, were a far cry from the service many in the regiment had expected, but events soon placed the 9th Vermont in the middle of one of the most disheartening Union defeats of the war.[6]

With his forces victorious after the Battle of Second Manassas, General Robert E. Lee and the Army of Northern Virginia would embark on a bold move northward into Maryland. In order to prevent the spread out garrisons in the area from being isolated, Union commanders ordered a consolidation of forces at Harpers Ferry, Virginia (now West Virginia). In compliance with the orders, the Union

---

[6] Ibid. 187.

forces at Winchester, including the 9th Vermont, abandoned the town and entered Harpers Ferry on September 3, 1862.[7] Nine days later, on September 12, Confederates under the command of Thomas J. "Stonewall" Jackson converged on Harpers Ferry and eventually surrounded the Union forces in the town.

The next three days would see sharp fighting, but by September 15, Colonel Dixon Miles, commander of the Union forces at Harpers Ferry, was compelled to surrender to Jackson. Colonel Stannard and the 9th Vermont, unwilling to accept surrender, attempted to escape through the Confederate lines, but the attempt was quickly discovered and foiled.[8] The 9th Vermont, along with over 12,000 other Union troops, became prisoners of war, and gained the dubious distinction of being part of the largest surrender of Union troops during the Civil War. The Union prisoners of war were soon paroled by Confederate forces with the understanding that they

---

[7] *Benedict*, 188.

[8] Paul G. Zeller. *The Ninth Vermont Infantry, A History and Roster* (Jefferson, NC: McFarland & Company, Inc., Publishers, 2008) 50. (Hereafter cited as *Zeller*).

would not take up arms again until properly exchanged at a later date.

It was during this period, awaiting exchange, that the 9th Vermont was sent to Camp Douglas in Chicago, Illinois to guard Confederate prisoners. In early March, Colonel Stannard was assigned command of a brigade of Vermont infantry, and Lieutenant Colonel Dudley K. Andross was promoted as the new colonel of the 9th Vermont.[9] Colonel Andross commanded the regiment for a little over two months before he resigned as colonel, and was replaced by Edward H. Ripley, now appointed to colonel from lieutenant colonel.[10] Colonel Edward Ripley was twenty-three years old at the time of the promotion.

The 9th Vermont would remain at Camp Douglas until exchanged on March 28, 1863; along with the exchange the regiment received orders sending them back to Virginia, eventually being posted in Suffolk. The 9th Vermont took part in three weeks of skirmishing with Confederate forces under Major General James Longstreet from the middle of

---

[9] *Zeller*, 75

[10] Ibid. 226

April until early May of 1863. When Longstreet withdrew his forces the 9th Vermont was moved to Yorktown in June, where it remained for the summer.[11] In October of 1863, the regiment was ordered to move from Yorktown to North Carolina due to the outbreak of malarial fevers. The move to a healthier climate was welcome news to the regiment, and a cause for optimism after the disappointments and setbacks in 1862 and 1863.

After arriving at Newport Barracks, Colonel Edward Ripley of the 9th Vermont was placed in overall command of the post and charged with defending the approaches to Morehead City and Beaufort from the west. In one of his first acts in command, Ripley ordered that the defensive works at Newport Barracks, which had been neglected, be improved. The defenses in the area were described as follows:

> The village of Newport was on the north side of the Newport River, a deep, unfordable stream emptying into the Neuse. The barracks were on the opposite side of the river, half a

---

[11] *Benedict*, 216

> mile from the village, and midway between the bridge by which the "county road" or highway between New Berne and Morehead City crossed the river and the railroad bridge half a mile farther down. The main defense of the camp was a redoubt armed with a 32- pound gun and three 12- pounders. On the coast road, leading along the shore of Bogue Sound, at a point about three miles from the barracks, was a blockhouse, and a picket line extended from this to a point on Gales Creek, seven miles west of the barracks, and thence to the swamps bordering the river- a circuit of twelve or fifteen miles.[12]

Included in the defenses were the main earthworks at Newport Barracks, an earthen redoubt at Shepardsville across the river from the barracks, and the outpost at Canady's Mill.

To the men in the 9th Vermont, service at Newport Barracks proved to be an unforgettable experience, as it was said the "moss-hung sycamore trees, the alligators and moccasin and copperhead snakes, the snuff-dipping natives, and the hunting of possums gave new scenes and occupations to the Vermonters.[13]" First Lieutenant Alfred C. Ballard, of Company B, provided a description of the land and one of the local delicacies:

---

[12] *Benedict*, 222-223

[13] *Ibid.* 223.

This is not good farming country. It is very level and sandy. Not a hill can be seen; nothing but the omnipresent pitch pines, which the people call "Turpentine Orchards," and which are the chief source of revenue. Sweet potatoes will grow here, a little cotton and corn and now and then a few peanuts. There is but little fruit here, not even a blackberry, though the soldiers do raise now and then a few apples, at seven dollars a barrel. Sweet potatoes are quite an item in the domestic economy of this section, as will appear from the following fact. The Captain and myself made an evening call not long since, at the home of one of the "F.F.N.C.'s," (First Families of North Carolina) and after roasting some of the potatoes in the fireplace, they peeled them, and passed them round, all hot and smoking and soft and sticky. We took each our potato in our fingers and gnaws them with becoming grace.

I am told the common way of waiting on people is to poke them potatoes out of the ashes with the toes of the boot, kick them towards you, and say, "help yourself"; but the Captain and I were evidently more refined people. [14]

Lieutenant Colonel of the 9th Vermont, Valentine G. Barney, would write that "this is a great country for a poor man to live in." He would continue: "wood costs nothing, Houses but little, Clothing but little, & game

---

[14] Donald H. Wickman. *Letters to Vermont, Volume II* (Bennington, VT: Images of the Past, 1998) 114. (Hereafter cited as *Letters*)

of all kinds is plenty." Barney, in addition, made note of the abundance of oysters and fish.[15]

Soldiers in the 9th Vermont in letters home were quite uncomplimentary of the local populace living in and around Newport Barracks. An anonymous writer would describe the people in the area:

> The men are lean, sallow complexioned, stoop-shouldered and indolent. The women are slovenly and grossly addicted to snuff dipping, and all alike, men, women and children are ignorant and contented.[16]

Captain Linus Sherman would be even harsher in his description of the local women as "lax in their style of dress, lax in housekeeping & loose in morals and everything else.[17]" Soon after arriving at Newport Barracks with the regiment, Captain Edwin Kilbourne wrote:

---

[15] Don Wickman. *"We Are Coming Father Abra'am" The History of the 9th Vermont Volunteer Infantry 1862-1865* (Lynchburg, VA: Schroeder Publications, 2005) 260-261. (Hereafter cited as *Wickman*)

[16] Ibid, 261.

[17] *Zeller,* 117.

> I haven't seen but 2 natives since landing here and they are fine specimens of the genus homo. Fine types of the poorer class of people which live and inhabit this southern clime. They are much below the African in intelligence and native wit and powers. In fact they are not to be put on the level with a *good intelligent horse.*[18]

No letters or diaries from the citizens around Newport Barracks have been found, but one might assume, if they were, that the descriptions might have been as equally unflattering in sentiment.

The routine of garrison duty in and around Newport Barracks was broken up from time to time by raids against Confederate held areas in Onslow and Jones County, or the occasional skirmish with Confederate cavalry or guerillas in the area.

On December 1, 1863, the 9th Vermont would suffer the loss of the highly popular Major Charles Jarvis, who was mortally wounded by a gunshot wound in the abdomen, during an encounter with Confederate cavalry near Cedar Point in Carteret County. After the Confederate who shot him was

---

[18] Ibid.

captured, the men of the party, led by Jarvis, asked if they should kill him on the spot, but Jarvis ordered against it stating that "no, he is a solider- take him prisoner," sparing the life of the young soldier who moments earlier had mortally wounded him. Jarvis died from his wound around 10 p.m. in a house near where he was wounded. Colonel Edward Ripley would write that "there is a settled, subdued air of sadness all about us tonight though out the command; such a one as I have never known before under circumstances of the kind."[19]

Compared with duty on more active fronts, the service at Newport Barracks could be described as routine and mundane. Joining the 9th Vermont would be the 23rd New York Cavalry, who assisted in scouting and picketing, and Company D of the 2nd Massachusetts Heavy Artillery, who manned the artillery at Newport Barracks.

The 23rd New York Cavalry was mustered into service between January and May of 1863, with

---

[19] *The New York Times*, December 23, 1863. New York, New York.

enlistments lasting for a period of three years. The organization of the regiment was never fully completed, with only two companies ever being raised. Company A was recruited from Lancaster, Tonawanda, Aurora, LeRoy, Colden, Pavilion, Bethany, Newstead, and Chicktawauga; with Company B being recruited from New York City.[20] The 23rd New York Cavalry left New York for North Carolina in May of 1863 and once there was assigned to the Department of North Carolina. Since the 23rd New York only consisted of two companies, a good portion of their service was spent attached to the 12th New York Cavalry.

The 23rd New York Cavalry was originally commanded by Lieutenant Colonel John H. Mix and the unit would often be referred to as "Mix's New Cavalry" or "Mix's Cavalry Battalion." In August of 1863, Lieutenant Colonel Mix was transferred out of the unit and command fell to Captain Emory

---

[20] Frederick Phisterer. *New York in the War of the Rebellion 1861-1865* (Albany: Weed, Parsons and Company, 1890) 320.

Cummings, who commanded the 23rd New York Cavalry during the fighting on February 2, 1864.[21]

Colonel Edward Ripley, writing in regards to the 23rd New York Cavalry, found the cavalrymen to be "lawless and undisciplined.[22]" Ripley's assessment aside, the 23rd New York did have some level of experience. In July of 1863, they had played an active role in Potter's cavalry raid in eastern North Carolina. Captain Cummings, during the raid, burned a river steamer, the *Governor Morehead,* near Tarboro and would be wounded by a fall from his horse, after it had been shot and killed, during a skirmish at Otter Creek during the raid.[23]

On the morning of February 2, 1864, it would be the pickets from the 23rd New York Cavalry that would be the first Union forces attacked by James Martin and his Confederates.

---

[21] David A. Norris. *Potter's Raid: The Union Cavalry's Boldest Expedition in Eastern North Carolina* (Wilmington, NC, Dram Tree Books, 2008) 25-26. (Hereafter cited as *Norris*)

[22] *Wickman*, 260.

[23] *Norris*, 94 and 120.

The 2nd Massachusetts Heavy Artillery was originally organized to be a veteran regiment, whose ranks would have been composed by soldiers whose nine-month enlistments were close to running out. Unfortunately the expected number of veterans reenlisting was not enough to fill the ranks and the companies became a mixture of veteran and green soldiers. Mustering of the regiment began in May of 1863, with Company D being mustered into service between July and August at Camp Meigs, in Reidville, Massachusetts.

On September 5, 1863, the first four companies of the 2nd Massachusetts Heavy Artillery departed Boston, bound for New Bern. These units would man the artillery at outposts and fortifications in the region. The companies routinely rotated throughout the New Bern area and in February of 1864, Company D was assigned to Newport Barracks under the command of Captain Russell H. Conwell.[24]

---

[24] Adjutant General of the State of Massachusetts. *Massachusetts Soldiers, Sailors, and Marines in the Civil War*. Volume Two. (Norwood, MA: Norwood, 1931.) 1241.

Overall, despite some members of the 9th Vermont and 23rd New York Cavalry seeing combat, many of the Union troops at Newport Barracks lacked experience under fire with many new recruits filling the ranks of the various units. February 2, 1864 would provide on-the-job training of the most serious nature. As would be seen, some units rose to the occasion and others performed quite woefully.

Chapter Four

"A very long and fatiguing but energetic march..."

Since January 19, 1864, many of the men of the 42nd North Carolina were tasked with building and strengthening fortifications near Virginia Creek, a point twenty-four miles from Wilmington along the road to New Bern. The company record of events for Company E of the 42nd stated that "this company, with the balance of the regiment, was ordered to the fortifications on Virginia Creek and remained there being severely exercised in "Irish Drill.[1]" As the men of his brigade continued working on fortifications, Brigadier General James G. Martin would head to Goldsboro to meet with Brigadier General Robert Hoke to discuss the upcoming plans for the attack on New Bern by Confederate forces converging at Kinston. Martin, in his report after the Battle of

---

[1] Supplement of the Official Records, Volume 49, 208. (Hereafter cited as *Supplement)*

Newport Barracks, would describe this meeting as a "short interview" with Hoke.[2]

Soon, Martin returned to Wilmington to organize the soldiers under his command for the upcoming operations in support of the main Confederate attack at New Bern. The role, requested of Martin and his command, required the coordination of forces spread out across the Department of the Cape Fear, as well as a rapid forced march towards the Union positions at Newport Barracks, but if a commander was suited to carry out such orders it was Martin.

On the morning and into the early afternoon of January 28, Martin with parts of the 17th and 42nd North Carolina left Wilmington on a march that would ultimately take them to battle against Union troops at Newport Barracks. Martin, in his report on the operations addressed to Major General W.H.C. Whiting at Wilmington, wrote:

> I left this city on Thursday, January 28, by direction of General Whiting, with parts of the Seventeenth and Forty-second

---

[2] *Official Records*, 84.

Regiments North Carolina troops. The next day the command was increased by a company of cavalry (Captain Harlan's), a battery of six guns under Captain Paris, two companies of the Seventeenth who were on picket at Topsail, and the remainder of the Forty-second, which had been at work on the fortifications at Virginia Creek.[3]

The next day Martin sent the following dispatch to Brigadier General Seth Barton:

> General: My command (two regiments and a battery) will be here to-night and at Jacksonville, 19 miles hence, about noon to-morrow. Thence I shall move to White Oak (Smith's Mill), where I hope to receive some information or directions as to my further movements, especially as to time.[4]

Martin and his troops reached Jacksonville on January 30, crossing the wagons and artillery using a single flat over the New River and the next morning continuing on to the White Oak River.

The afternoon of January 31, while at the White Oak River, near Smith's Mill, saw Martin's command

---

[3] *Official Records*,84. The cavalry mentioned was Company K of the 5th South Carolina Cavalry. Captain Paris' battery refers to the Staunton Hill Artillery.

[4] Ibid. 87.

for the first time in the operation at full strength. In his report, Martin wrote that "At this point Colonel Jackson, with the remaining four companies of the Seventeenth, one battery of artillery, and parts of three companies of cavalry, joined the command.[5]" Colonel George Jackson, under orders from Martin, had marched the remainder of the Confederate force from Kenansville. With the arrival of the additional troops, Martin would have around 2500 men under his command. Jackson, a Virginian, before the outbreak of war, had served as a lieutenant in the 2nd United States Cavalry then commanded by Robert E. Lee.[6]

Around this time, Martin would receive a dispatch with additional instructions from Barton:

> General: All goes smoothly with us. You will hear us at work in the morning. I am afraid you will not reach the point designated by Pickett at the time we expected; nevertheless, push

---

[5] Ibid. 84. This force included Company A of the 3rd Battalion North Carolina Light Artillery and Company E of the 5th North Carolina Cavalry.

[6] *Moore*, 255. Jackson, in addition to serving with Lee, was the cousin of Thomas J. "Stonewall" Jackson.

on and reach there as quickly as possible. I will keep you advised.[7]

Martin ordered pickets to move out on each side of the White Oak River with orders to "arrest every person moving about.[8]" No chances would be taken to allow the Union forces in the area to be made aware of the presence of Martin and his forces.

After the pickets were sent across the White Oak River, Martin and his troops were tasked with bridging the river, as the previous bridge at the crossing had been destroyed. Martin wrote in his report that "Captain Starke, acting brigade inspector, was at once set to work with a strong party to bridge the river. This work required nearly the whole night.[9]" The bridge that Starke and the work detail built was constructed with pine trees without the use of nails.[10] Early the next morning, on Monday February 1, Martin and his command began crossing over the White Oak River. Around 8 a.m., Martin

---

[7] *Official Records*, 87.

[8] Ibid. 84.

[9] Ibid. Martin and his soldiers used this bridge on their march back to Wilmington after the Battle of Newport Barracks.

[10] Southern Historical Society Papers, Volume XXIII, 190.

composed his last dispatch to Barton before the battle of February 2:

> General: My artillery is now crossing the bridge I had made last night. If for any reason you fall back inform me promptly, as my rear is entirely uncovered except by your force. I leave couriers on the road. It is 40 miles hence to Sheppardsville. Please keep me informed. I have not yet heard your guns.[11]

The march of February 1 was described in great detail in the Company Report of the 17th North Carolina:

> Crossed the river in the morning with the whole command. My company, Company B, and the cavalry were sent forward as advance guard. We touched Jones Co. and entered Carteret that day. Marched to within about twelve or fifteen miles of Shepherdsville, a depot on the Atlantic and North Carolina Railroad. Camped for the night and fared sumptuously on cheese and molasses we took during the day from disloyal citizens coming from the picket post.[12]

---

[11] *Official Records*, 87.

[12] *Supplement*, 712. In the edited version of the Supplement to the Official Records, Jones County was incorrectly transcribed from the original as "Jones' Company". Based on a closer look at

While the men of Company D of the 17th North Carolina were partaking in cheese and molasses, Brigadier General James G. Martin prepared for the expected fighting that would follow on the next day. The Confederate forces were the recipients of a bit of good luck in the form of a Union deserter captured during the day on February 1. *The Carolina Watchman* from Salisbury, North Carolina reported that "our cavalry advance picked up a Yankee, who had deserted the night previous. From him Gen. Martin obtained full information of the enemy's forces, the number of guns he had, and the position of the block-houses and forts.[13]" Martin later wrote:

> During the day caught a deserter from the enemy and derived from him valuable information of the position, strength, and condition of the enemy, on which I acted and all of which was true. I am of the opinion this man should be treated differently from the other prisoners.[14]

---

the original copy of the document and based on the context of the sentence, the transcribed version should read Jones County.

13 *The Carolina Watchman Weekly*, March 7, 1864, Salisbury, North Carolina. (Hereafter cited as *Carolina Watchman* from the date of publication, unless otherwise noted)

14 *Official Records*, 85.

That evening it began to rain, and worried over the condition of the dirt roads his troops would be marching over, Martin ordered that any wagons and transportation that could be spared be sent back over the White Oak River.[15] Unknown to the Union forces in the area, the Confederates were camped just a short distance from the Gales Creek Blockhouse.

It was a march of around 110 miles covered in only five days. Martin and his troops covered on average about twenty miles a day over roads that were "heavy sandy roads at this end of the line, and deep muddy ones at the other.[16]" After the war, it would be described as being a "very long and fatiguing but energetic march, most skillfully concealed from the enemy.[17]" A participant in the ranks recounted a few weeks later:

> That night we encamped fourteen miles from Shepardsville, in a dense swamp, whose murkiness and gloom were increased, if possible, by a rain which fell through the night.

---

[15] Ibid.

[16] *The Wilmington Journal*, February 11, 1864, Wilmington, North Carolina. (Hereafter cited as *Wilmington Journal*)

[17] Southern Historical Papers, Volume XXIII, 189.

Nothwithstanding the forced march of the previous day, and the discomfort of the night, the troops rose with cheerfulness and alacrity, and prepared for the day's toilsome march, and for battle.[18]

[18] *Carolina Watchman Weekly*, March 7, 1864

Chapter Five

"The Cavalry Dashed Furiously Forward..."

Early on the rainy morning of Tuesday February 2, Brigadier General James Martin started his command on the march and towards the fighting that the day undoubtedly had in store. As Martin and his Confederates moved ever closer, Captain James Gorman and the Union troops under his command at the Gales Creek Blockhouse prepared for another day of routine picket duty. As would soon be seen, this day would hold nothing of the monotony that Gorman and his men had become accustomed to.

Gales Creek was a small, but prosperous, community in western Carteret County sitting off of the Cedar Point Road. Located nearby was the landing at Gales Creek, where small boats loaded and unloaded goods. From there roads headed west and northwest towards Swansboro, White Oak, and Pollocksville, and east to Carolina City and Morehead City. Another road veered off in the direction of Shepardsville and the main Union force located at

Newport Barracks, four miles away. The defenses erected by Union troops at Gales Creek consisted of a wooden blockhouse and earthworks to guard the approaches to Gales Creek from the east and west; in addition to the defenses a small church and meeting house were used as a headquarters and barracks.[1]

Captain Gorman had under his command at Gales Creek the sixty men of his Company H of the 9th Vermont and a detachment of cavalry from Company A of the 23rd New York Cavalry, around twenty-five men. Of the sixty men in Company H, forty-three were new recruits recently arrived to the regiment and of those only two-thirds were actually armed with muskets.[2] That morning Gorman deployed his men in three lines. The first line was two miles west of Gales Creek and consisted of the twenty-five men from the 23rd New York Cavalry, who were tasked with picketing the roads and approaches from Gales Creek to the White Oak River. The second and third lines were composed of soldiers from Company H. The second line was advanced a few hundred yards from the main line, which was located at the blockhouse.

---

[1] *Poheresky*, 9

[2] *Wickman*, 275

Captain Gorman and the eighty-five men under his command would soon be met head on by the advance force of around 2500 Confederates heading directly towards their position.

After breaking camp, the Confederate line of march, divided into two columns, advanced down a small road that led from Peletier's Mills to Gales Creek. The first column was an advance guard under the command of Colonel George Jackson that consisted of two companies from the 17th North Carolina and one from the 42nd North Carolina. Along with the three companies of infantry were the four guns of Captain Andrew Ellis from Company A of the 3rd Battalion North Carolina Light Artillery and all of the cavalry in Martin's force under the command of Lieutenant Colonel Jeffords of the 5th South Carolina Cavalry.

The rest of Martin's command followed in the second column in the following order: the 17th North Carolina, the 42nd North Carolina, and the Staunton Hill (Virginia) Artillery. The supply train and rear guard rounded out Martin's line of march.[3] The role

---

3 *Official Records*, 85

of the advance guard that morning was to screen or "feel" for the enemy; if contact was made the cavalry and infantry could move forward to engage or allow the main column of infantry the time to deploy into a line of battle. Ellis with his guns would provide the counter-battery fire on any Union gun positions or entrenchments along the route. Martin, as it would be seen, would make excellent use of this formation.

Captain John L. Swain from Company E of the 17th North Carolina recalled in his diary entry of February 12, 1864, the words of General Martin as he rode past the marching Confederates:

> Soldiers, you hear the guns of General Lee. He has come to take New Berne and he has sent you down here to take this camp and cut off supplies and he expects you will do it. "We will, we will" cried Lieutenant Colonel Lamb.[4]

Around 8 a.m., Martin and his command first discovered the Union pickets of the 23rd New York

---

4 Christopher M. Watford, editor. *The Civil War in North Carolina: Soldier's and Civilian's Letters and Diaries, 1861-1865: Volume 2, The Mountains* (Jefferson, NC: McFarland and Company, Inc., Publishers, 2003) 149.

Cavalry around six to seven miles away from Newport Barracks. The Confederate cavalry, before attacking, were given "strict orders" not to fire their weapons "for fear of alarming the enemy."[5] The initial fighting of the day was described as follows:

> On nearing the first pickets of the enemy and discovering them on the alert, the cavalry dashed furiously forward, and the Yankee pickets (twenty-five or thirty in number) retreated as fast as their horses would carry them. The road over which pursuers and pursued had to pass was through a swamp and full of deep holes overflowing with mud and water. But on they sped- some of the Yankee horses and their riders turning somersaults in the mud, and ours running over them, and tumbling headlong into the deep mire after them, inflicting many bruises upon men and horses (breaking the neck of one of the latter) but doing no serious damage to the riders.[6]

Some of the injuries though were much more serious than bumps and bruises. As the Union cavalry fell back it was reported that the lieutenant in charge of the pickets suffered a "saber cut to the shoulder."[7] Along with the wounded lieutenant, four members of

---

5 *Carolina Watchman*, March 7, 1864

6 *Wilmington Journal*, February 11, 1864.

7 *Benedict*, 227

Company A of the 23rd Cavalry were captured in the initial charge of the Confederate cavalry. Corporals William Boller, Charles Chappell, and Jefferson Moore, along with Private Walter Ross, fell into Confederate hands during the retreat back towards the Gales Creek Blockhouse, all would be sent to Confederate prison camps. Corporal William Boller and Private Walter Ross were sent to Andersonville Prison in Georgia. Ross, twenty-two years old, would die of disease on September 8, 1864 with Boller, twenty-six years old, passing away only a few days later on September 16, 1864.[8]

The attacking Confederates were also not immune from casualties in the charge. First Lieutenant Noah F. Muse, of Company E of the 5th North Carolina Cavalry, was likely the first man killed that day. One account of his death states that he was "killed just as he was in the act of striking his enemy." The account continues that "his blow fell, wounding the enemy, apparently after he himself had been

[8] Service Records of William Boller, Charles Chappell, Jefferson Moore and Walter Ross of 23rd New York Cavalry. Located at The National Archives in Washington, D.C.

killed."[9] *The Wilmington Journal* on February 11, 1864 would report that Muse "while gallantly leading the charge, fell mortally wounded by a pistol shot from a Yankee who was being hotly pursued."[10] It was said of Muse that "he was beloved by all how knew him, he nobly gave his young life to this country."[11] The Company Report from Company A of the 23rd New York Cavalry notes that the Confederates lost a "lieutenant killed, four privates wounded."[12]

After falling back to the main force located at the blockhouse the men of the 23rd New York would ride on to Newport Barracks to alert the command there of the presence of a large force of Confederates advancing towards them.[13] This report from the 23rd New York Cavalry would be the first indication any Union troops in the region had that Martin and his Confederates were near.

---

9 *Official Records*, 85.

10 *Wilmington Journal*, February 11, 1864

11 *Carolina Watchman*, March 7, 1864

12 *Supplement*, Volume 41, 695

13 *Wickman*, 275.

By 9 a.m., the Confederate advance guard deployed and moved against Company H of the 9th Vermont at the Gales Creek Blockhouse. As the Confederates moved closer to the position, Captain Gorham ordered the unarmed men of his command to fall back to the Bogue Sound Blockhouse three miles away. Many of these men, new recruits, not familiar with the lay of the land in the area, would become lost and later captured before they reached the Bogue Sound Blockhouse.[14]

After sweeping away the Union cavalry pickets the Confederate advance guard pushed on towards the infantry located at the Gales Creek Blockhouse. Confederate sources do not indicate if it was the cavalry or infantry of Martin's command that first attacked the pickets of Company H. In fact, according to the official report of James Martin, after the initial attack by his cavalry, the advance guard moved "steadily and quickly towards forward and soon came to the first block-house, which was hurriedly left by the enemy after a few discharges from our artillery."[15]

---

[14] *Wickman*, 275.

[15] *Official Records,* 85.

Another Confederate account written a few days after the battle states that:

> Having captured a portion and dispersed the rest of these out-post pickets, the column moved forward and soon came to a trading post of the Yankees- but the enemy had fled in the direction of a blockhouse some half mile distant- pickets and reserves. The march was continued and preparations made to storm the work, but a close examination disclosed the fact that the position had been evacuated by the enemy in such hot haste that they left their provisions, books, letters, &c., behind them.[16]

A Union account written after the war of the action recounts:

> The infantry pickets next came in, less a dozen of their number who had been cut off and captured; but not without having inflicted some loss upon the enemy. One of the new recruits, Oberon Payne by name, shot a mounted man, supposed to be an officer, from his horse, and the animal, keeping on, came within reach of the pickets and was brought in with the empty saddle.[17]

---

[16] *Wilmington Journal*, February 11, 1864

[17] *Benedict*, 227. There is the possibility that the mounted man Payne is stated to have shot could have been Lieutenant Noah Muse of the 5th NC Cavalry.

These accounts seem to suggest that the Confederate cavalry continued their pursuit of the Union cavalry pickets up to the second line of Union troops that contained the pickets of Company H of the 9th Vermont. With the presence of Union infantry, the North Carolina and South Carolina cavalrymen pulled back as the infantry and artillery of Martin's advance guard moved forward towards the blockhouse. It is likely at this point Captain Andrew Ellis and his gunners from Company A of the 3rd Battalion North Carolina Light Artillery unlimbered and fired the "few discharges" from their artillery pieces that Martin mentioned in his report.[18]

As the three companies of infantry from the 17th and 42nd North Carolina advanced quickly towards the pickets of Company H, Captain Gorman ordered the men to fall back to the main line located at the blockhouse, but before they fell back they fired a volley into the oncoming Confederate infantry and then hastily fell back, under the cloud of white smoke from their volley.[19]

---

[18] *Official Records*, 85.

[19] *Zeller,* 131.

With the pickets back at the blockhouse, Captain Gorman prepared his men to meet the Confederate attack. Unfortunately for Gorman and his men they were greatly outnumbered by the attacking Confederates, so any stand made at the Gales Creek Blockhouse would be temporary one as Gorman's force at this point numbered around only forty-five to fifty men (the unarmed men of his command previously being sent away at the start of the fighting). It can be estimated that the advance guard of Martin's force outnumbered Gorman and his men at a ratio of four to one.

With the odds clearly not in favor of the men from Vermont, Gorman ordered his men to fire one more volley into the Confederates before abandoning the position and retreating to a nearby wood line.[20] This would be a fighting retreat as Gorman and his men "fell back slowly, stopping frequently to fire, and holding the enemy's skirmishers in check."[21] It was during this portion of the fight that twenty-four year old Private Stephen Burrows was wounded in the left

---

[20] *Wickman*, 276.

[21] *Benedict*, 228.

hand by a Confederate bullet. Burrows bandaged his hand and continued to fall back with his comrades.[22] The Confederate infantry continued to push towards the wood line where the remaining men of Company H made one last, brief, stand before using the cover of the dense woods to cover their retreat back towards Newport Barracks. The remains of Captain Gorman's Company H would reach Newport Barracks later that day.[23]

From the time the pickets from Company A of the 23rd New York Cavalry were first attacked, to the retreat of Company H of the 9th Vermont back towards Newport Barracks, the fighting at the Gales Creek Blockhouse lasted about two hours from 8 a.m. to 10 a.m. that morning. Due to the rapid pace of the fighting casualties from this portion of the battle are somewhat difficult to compile. Confederate losses were one killed, with the report of four privates wounded. Union losses in the two units engaged were two men wounded and sixteen captured. Of the

---

[22] *Zeller*, 131. Burrows, after reaching a hospital, would see his index, middle, and part of his ring finger amputated. He was ultimately discharged on December 16, 1864, due to this wound.

[23] *Benedict*, 228.

sixteen men captured, nine would ultimately perish in as prisoners of war in Confederate prison camps.

After forcing the Union troops defending the Gales Creek Blockhouse to retreat back to Newport Barracks, Brigadier General James Martin ordered the blockhouse and meeting house destroyed. After what was described by one Confederate as an "exciting little episode," Martin and his men resumed their march towards the next target of the day, the Bogue Sound Blockhouse, located four miles away.[24]

---

24 *Carolina Watchman.* March 7, 1864

Chapter Six

"A Spirited Resistance"

Shortly after 10am, Brigadier General James Martin and his Confederate forces marched down the Sound Road, moving in the direction of the Bogue Sound Blockhouse. Standing in the way of Martin were the men of Company B of the 9th Vermont under the command of First Lieutenant Alfred C. Ballard. Ballard had under his command sixty-two men, "half of them recruits who had received their guns and a pocket-full of cartridges apiece that morning.[1]"

A Confederate advancing that morning described the area of the advance to *The Carolina Watchman Weekly* newspaper in Salisbury, North Carolina as follows:

> In some countries there can be found some dry land even in the midst of swamps, but your correspondent will defy the most critical observer to find any within four miles of Shepardsville. An endless succession of dark, dreary swamps, whose only growth is the bamboo brier, and the laurel, mark a

---

[1] *Benedict*, 228

country which, were it not ours, none but the Yankees should ever inhabit.[2]

Like their fellow soldiers from Company H, the troops of Company B were outnumbered by overwhelming odds. But, to their advantage, the Bogue Sound Blockhouse offered a stronger defensive position than the Gales Creek Blockhouse, with its rifle pits and a howitzer mounted on a naval carriage in the blockhouse itself.[3]

Around 11am, the fighting around the Bogue Sound Blockhouse began, but the exact details of how it began are murky. It is not clear if the men of Company B had heard the fighting earlier that morning at the Gales Creek Blockhouse. Evidence seems to suggest that none of the unarmed men of Company H who had been ordered to fall back to the Bogue Sound Blockhouse by Captain Gorman ever reached that post, either captured or lost among the unfamiliar territory. Whether or not they heard the fighting at Gales Creek, very soon the men of

---

[2] *Carolina Watchman,* March 7, 1864

[3] *Wickman*, 277.

Company B learned of the presence of Confederate troops. As to the matter of who started the fighting at the Bogue Sound Blockhouse, that is a matter of speculation, but a few accounts do shed some light on the question.

Lieutenant Alfred Ballard, commander of Company B of the 9th Vermont, writing nine days after the fighting would state that "the enemy opened up on the Block House with three pieces of artillery."[4] A post-war Union account described that "the enemy appeared to company B at the block-house about eleven o'clock, making his presence known by a solid shot which went through the block-house."[5] These accounts support the idea that the Confederate artillery of Captain Andrew Ellis and his battery of guns from Company A of the 3rd Battalion North Carolina Light Artillery unlimbered and opened fire first on the Union position.

But an account from *The Wilmington Journal* on February 11, 1864, by a participant in the fighting, describes the opening of the fighting at the Bogue Sound Blockhouse in a different light:

---

4 *Letters*, 116.

5 *Benedict*, 228.

Continuing the march for two and a half miles further, a second blockhouse was discovered, and our forces were brought to a stand by a shot from a six-pounder which went whizzing over their heads. No one knew the strength of the place- how much infantry or artillery constituted the garrison. It was easily discovered that it was a well-built, thick walled house, surrounded by a circumvallation of earth works.[6]

Brigadier General Martin, in his official report stated:

About 4 miles farther came to the second block-house, at the junction of the main sound road to Morehead City and the road to Newport Barracks (distant about 4 miles). In this block-house was a piece of artillery and the enemy indicated an intention to hold it. The artillery of the advance had already opened fire upon it when I came up.[7]

The account from *The Wilmington Journal* and the official report of Brigadier General Martin, seem to point to the men of Company B of the 9th Vermont firing first. While the record is not clear on who opened fire first, it is clear on the fact that an artillery

---

[6] *Wilmington Journal*, February 11, 1864

[7] *Official Records*, 85

duel between Captain Ellis with his gunners and the Union defenders of the Bogue Sound Blockhouse marked the opening actions of this portion of the fight.

Before the first shots were fired to signal the commencement of hostilities at the Bogue Sound Blockhouse, one Carteret County family found themselves in the midst of an impending battle. Levi T. Oglesby's sound-side home was surrounded that morning by Confederates forming for the attack on the Bogue Sound Blockhouse. Levi Oglesby had left that morning for Beaufort, but his wife and their six small children were still home. With their home in the path of the fighting, Mrs. Oglesby and her family were advised to move to a safer location.[8]

One of the slaves, named Homer Ward, owned by the Oglesby family, was working the fields near the home. Ward, clad in a blue shirt and cap, alarmed by the appearance of Confederate soldiers set off running

---

[8] *Captain Levi Tolson Oglesby* by L. Markham Hibbs, Jr. *The Researcher* published by the Carteret County Historical Society, Volume XXIII, Number 1 , Spring-Summer 2007, page 5. (Hereafter cited as *Oglesby*.)

towards an out building on the property. With his clothing resembling that of a Union soldier, Confederate troops demanded his surrender, and threatened to shoot him if he moved again. At this point Mrs. Oglesby cried "he's no Yankee," and ran out in front of the Confederates blocking their aim, evidently convincing them that Ward was not an enemy combatant.[9] Family tradition holds that Brigadier General James Martin, shortly after the incident, knelt beside his horse to pray near the Oglesby home. The family soon evacuated, fleeing to the home of a nearby relative, where they would spend the night of February 2.[10]

With the artillery of his command engaged with the howitzer of the Bogue Sound Blockhouse, Brigadier General Martin ordered an infantry company of his advance guard up to assault and capture the Bogue Sound Blockhouse. Martin recounts his order to commit the infantry into the fight:

---

9 Ibid. 6.

10 Ibid.

> A Company of the Seventeenth, well instructed as skirmishers, was once thrown forward under the fire of our artillery, with orders to take it if practicable. Captain Biggs' company was designated for this attack. Lieutenant Hassell, acting brigade ordinance officer, belonging to this company, asked and received permission to join it for this service.[11]

Unfortunately, there is no approximation of the length of the artillery duel, or the time it took Brigadier General Martin to order in the infantry for the assault on the blockhouse.

As Company A of the 17th North Carolina moved forward as skirmishers commanded by Captain William Biggs, Lieutenant Ballard and the men of Company B of the 9th Vermont stood resolutely, determined "not to be gobbled up so easily."[12] As the skirmishers from the 17th North Carolina reached within two hundred yards of the Union position, the order was given to charge the works with the men of the 17th advancing with "the alacrity of volunteers and the steadiness of regulars;" Ballard and his men opened fire with their muskets as

---

[11] *Official Records*, 85.

[12] *Letters*, 116.

the rushing North Carolinians responded "with a yell which rang out amid the volleys of musketry."[13] The Vermonters of Company B gave the men of the 17th North Carolina "a very warm reception" and inflicted some casualties on the attackers.[14] The skirmishers were temporarily stunned and their advance halted, but soon Company A of the 17th North Carolina regrouped under Captain Biggs and continued forward.

As the North Carolinians moved closer, the tenuousness of Company B's position at the Bogue Sound Blockhouse increased with each passing moment. As the men of the 17th North Carolina pushed on to the blockhouse, they closed the road to Newport Barracks, leaving Ballard the Sound Road back to Morehead City as the only route of retreat. With Confederate troops nearly surrounding the Bogue Sound Blockhouse, and after a "spirited resistance," Lieutenant Ballard issued the order to his command to retreat from the blockhouse or face certain capture. The last man of Company B to leave the Bogue Sound Blockhouse was twenty-one year old

---

13 *Wilmington Journal*, February 11, 1864

14 *Wickman*, 279.

Corporal Willard Sisco, who pulled the lanyard to fire one more round from the howitzer, before he leapt from the window and retreated.[15] With the order to retreat the men of Company B moved quickly from the blockhouse and rifle pits, all the while firing at the pursuing Confederates, and fell back towards Morehead City.[16]

It was during the withdrawal to Morehead City that the men of Company B, without the protection of the blockhouse or rifle pits, began to suffer casualties as Private William Smith, twenty-one years old, was wounded by a ricocheted bullet that fractured his skull. Private Nathan DeForge, thirty-eight years old, was wounded in the left leg. With the victorious Confederates closing in, both privates were left where they fell and captured. Due to the severity of their wounds, both men were paroled by the Confederates and left at a neighboring farmhouse, most likely the Oglesby home.[17]

Lieutenant Ballard, wrote a few days after the battle that the men of Company B "put for the woods

---

[15] Ibid. 279

[16] *Zeller*, 132

[17] Ibid.

at a very quick step, for the swarms of rebels were after us screaming and yelling as victorious soldiers know how to do."[18] Ballard would continue:

> Our escape from the rebels was most fortunate, as it appears on reviewing the affair. The Company was ordered to hold the place as long as possible, and it was held until some of the boys thought that the Lieutenant commanding was calculating to surrender the whole Company as prisoners, but such was not his plan. But it is generally believed that if we had remained two minutes longer, all would have been taken, as the enemy were closing in on several sides.[19]

Along with the two wounded men, Company B lost eight men captured, four of which would later die in Confederate prison camps at Andersonville, Georgia and Salisbury, North Carolina.[20]

Brigadier General James Martin reported that after a "short delay" his men moved on towards Newport Barracks.[21] The reason for the delay, which Martin does not go into detail on, might have been to

---

[18] *Letters*, 116.

[19] Ibid.

[20] *Zeller*, 133

[21] *Official Records*, 85

restore order in his ranks. In the aftermath of the triumph at the Bogue Sound Blockhouse, it was reported that the Confederates captured "a beautiful six-pounder cannon, a number of rifles, knapsacks, clothing, commissary stores, and &c."[22] Undoubtedly, some time must have been spent collecting the military stores, but one might also assume that the victorious troops in Martin's ranks might have fallen out of line, without orders, to collect their own prizes from the victory.

Despite the reports of no losses in the action at the Bogue Sound Blockhouse, the Confederates seem to have suffered some casualties in the fighting. Union accounts point to such, and in the aftermath it was written that the slaves of the Oglesby family tended to the wounded of both sides in the kitchen of the Oglesby home.[23]

The next morning, the Oglesby family returned home to find their house in shambles. "All the food and clothing had been taken, including shoes. A small

---

[22] *Wilmington Journal,* February 11, 1864

[23] *Oglesby*, 6

amount of corn meal left in a container was all the food found."[24]

While successful for the second time that day, the day was far from over for Brigadier General Martin and his Confederates as "the principal work of the day was still to be done."[25] The primary target of the campaign, Newport Barracks and the railroad trestle there still loomed ahead only a few miles away.

---

[24] Ibid.

[25] *Wilmington Journal,* February 11, 1864

Chapter Seven

"Such a scurrying time you never saw..."

On February 1, the Confederate forces under Major General George Pickett began their attempt to recapture New Bern by attacking the Union forces garrisoned there. From the very start, the Confederates suffered from miscommunication and ran into unexpected obstacles. As the attack unraveled, Pickett and the Confederates under his command saw, with each passing moment of confusion and delay, their chances of success slipping away.

Private Lyman Chamberlain of the 27th Massachusetts, a hospital steward at the Hammond General Hospital in Beaufort would write that "we could hear the cannons roar, although it is a distance of forty miles from here."[1]

---

[1] The Civil War Letters of Private Lyman Chamberlain, Co. B – 27th Massachusetts Volunteer Regiment, 1862-1864. Letter Seventeen, from the library of The History Place in Morehead City, North Carolina. (Hereafter cited as *Chamberlain*)

The action at New Bern caused quite the stir in the military Sub-District of Beaufort, which included not only that town, but also Newport Barracks and adjacent outposts in Carteret County. Colonel James Jourdan of the 158th New York Infantry, commander of the Sub-District of Beaufort, undoubtedly heard the same firing as Private Chamberlain, and soon orders reached him from Brigadier General Innis Palmer in New Bern for assistance. Jourdan in his official report recounted his actions after he received his orders:

> On the 1st instant, in compliance with the orders from Brigadier General Palmer, I sent the One hundred and fifty-eighth Regiment New York State Volunteers to New Berne, leaving Morehead garrisoned by Company C, Second Massachusetts Heavy Artillery, and about 200 unarmed recruits of the One hundred and fifty-eighth New York State Volunteers. I withdrew 100 men from the garrison of Fort Macon, 50 of whom I placed at Beaufort. On the night of the 1st instant I received the arms and ammunition asked for, with which every man, both soldier and citizen, was armed for the defense of the place.[2]

As Colonel Jourdan shifted forces from his command to New Bern and around his sub-district,

---

[2] *Official Records,* 77

James Rumley, a Confederate sympathizer living in Beaufort, wrote in his diary wrote that "at 11 o'clock this morning, news reached this place from Morehead City that a telegraphic dispatch had just been received from New Bern, announcing the fact that Confederates had appeared in force around that town; that an attack was hourly expected; and calling for all disposable armed force at this post." Rumley continued in his diary that "the pickets around Beaufort have been hurriedly called in, and the troops are rapidly getting off for New Bern. Great excitement among the troops, Yankee citizens and negroes.[3]"

Mary von Olnhausen, a nurse serving in Morehead City, in a letter on February 5, 1864 wrote that the appearance of Confederates at New Bern and Carteret County caused quite a bit of confusion and panic in the town. She would go on to say that "such a scurrying time you never saw."[4] The sounds of battle

---

[3] Judkin Browning, editor. *The Southern Mind under Union Rule: The Diary of James Rumley, Beaufort, North Carolina, 1862-1865*, (University Press of Florida, 2009) 121. (Hereafter cited as *Southern Mind.*)

[4] James Phinney Munroe, editor. *Adventures of an Army Nurse in Two Wars: Edited from the Diary and Correspondence of Mary Phinney, Baroness von Olnhausen,* (Boston, MA: Little,

heard almost forty miles away in New Bern, would soon be heard again, but this time much closer.

Captain Russell H. Conwell, in command of Company D of the 2nd Massachusetts Heavy Artillery, on the night of February 1 had headed to Canady's Mill. On his return to Newport Barracks, Conwell was fired upon by an unknown shooter, barely escaping serious injury or death. The watch that Conwell was wearing in his breast pocket had luckily stopped the bullet. After reaching safety, Conwell reported to the commander of Newport Barracks Lieutenant Colonel Valentine Barney, in temporary command of the post, what had transpired. Barney ordered the next morning that Lieutenant John Whitcher, of Company G of the 9th Vermont, and twenty-five men accompany Conwell back to Canady's Mill to search out those responsible for the shooting. Whitcher was given orders to leave half his men at the site of the shooting, with the other half returning to Newport Barracks in

---

Brown, and Company, 1904) 133. (Hereafter cited as *Adventures of an Army Nurse*)

three hours. At 9 a.m. Conwell and the party led by Whitcher set off towards Canady's Mill.[5]

An hour later, at 10 a.m., a rider on horseback brought the news to Newport Barracks that the outpost at Gales Creek had been attacked by a Confederate force of unknown strength. With this news, Lieutenant Colonel Barney telegraphed Colonel Jourdan at Morehead City to alert him to the new developments taking place. Soon after, Barney and the men under his command heard the unmistakable sound of fighting coming from the direction of the Bogue Sound Blockhouse. While the sounds of battle certainly piqued the attention of some at Newport Barracks, one group of soldiers had their attention turned to another matter- the cooking of rabbit stew over the fire.[6]

After he received the telegraph from Newport Barracks, Colonel Jourdan boarded a train in Morehead City and proceeded west down the Atlantic

---

[5] *Zeller*, 133 Lieutenant Valentine Barney was in temporary command of the post at Newport Barracks while Colonel Edward Ripley was in Newport News, Virginia escorting Confederate prisoners to that location.

[6] *Wickman,* 276

and North Carolina Railroad. Jourdan arrived at Newport Barracks around 11 a.m. and immediately took control of the situation in consultation with Lieutenant Colonel Valentine Barney of the 9th Vermont. In his report Jourdan noted the orders he gave:

> As soon as I learned of the approach of the enemy in my front, I went to Newport Barracks per train, to give directions in reference to the defense of that place. I immediately withdrew the detachment at Kennedy's Mill to prevent their capture, and directed that the guns in the two forts should be used as long as possible, and if the abandonment of the fort was compelled, that the guns should be brought out and thrown in the Newport River; or if this were impossible they should be spiked and the wheels and carriages broken. They were to be saved, if at all possible, even should cavalry horses be used to drag them.[7]

It is unknown if Company E of the 9th Vermont stationed at Canady's Mill was fully aware of what was unfolding near there with the attacks of the Gales Creek and Bogue Sound Blockhouses, but the decision to pull them back from their post was quite prudent, preventing them from being cut off from the rest of

---

[7] *Official Records*, 78

the command. Jourdan issued further instructions as he described in his official report:

> I ordered Lieutenant-Colonel Barney, commanding officer of the post, to fight as long as possible, and if driven back to do so slowly, falling back on Morehead City, but if cut off in that direction, to fall back upon Newport village and there make a stand upon opposite bank of the river, destroying the bridges in his front. If driven back from there he would retreat to Beaufort.
>
> I took all the sick and part of the quartermaster's stores on board the train to Morehead City, leaving directions that at the last extremity, to prevent falling into the enemy's hands, all public stores then remaining to be burnt.[8]

After the sick and part of the quartermaster's stores were loaded on board the train, Colonel Jourdan headed back to attend to the defenses of Morehead City. Once again in Morehead City, Jourdan sent a telegraph to Brigadier General Palmer in New Bern apprising him of the developing situation around 1 p.m. His message to Palmer read:

> The enemy have taken Gale's Creek and Bogue Sound block-house. I have just come from the front. I am confident in my ability to hold the Morehead line about 10 miles about

---

[8] Ibid.

> Carolina City. The enemy is in strong force; the infantry is estimated about 2,000, what three pieces of artillery and a strong force of cavalry. Before the capture of the above post we repulsed them several times. I am afraid they will be captured. I have moved my sick to Morehead from Newport. I will use everything available to repulse them. I am moving all my little force, even convalescents, to the front. I am confident of success.[9]

The estimate of Confederate forces that Jourdan relayed to Palmer was surprisingly accurate in terms of actual numbers that Brigadier General James Martin had in the ranks that day. While not stated, it can be assumed that this accurate report was from the efficient intelligence gathering by the troopers from the 23rd New York Cavalry, who initially reported the Confederate attack at Gales Creek to Barney at Newport Barracks earlier that morning. Knowing the odds are greatly against the men at Newport Barracks, Lieutenant Colonel Barney and his troops grimly prepared to defend against the coming Confederate onslaught.

---

[9] Ibid. 80-81

Such long odds, even with veteran troops in the ranks, would give a commander pause, but with a force mostly composed of "green" and untested men the feelings that Lieutenant Colonel Valentine Barney felt must have bordered on trepidation as he prepared his command for battle. Despite any concerns Barney may have had, he was resolved to do his duty, and if compelled to fall back would not give up Newport Barracks without a fight. Barney ordered the regimental drummers to sound the long roll and soon the men under his command gathered their gear and fell in line.[10] With Barney in command of all Union troops at Newport Barracks, temporary command of the 9th Vermont fell to Captain Samuel H. Kelley of Company B.[11]

As Barney and Kelley prepared their men, the 9th Vermont had only seven of its ten companies present at Newport Barracks. Company H, posted at the Gales Creek Blockhouse, was retreating back to Newport Barracks but was disorganized and Company B, cut off from retreat back to Newport Barracks, was falling back to Morehead City. The remainder of the

---

[10] *Zeller*, 134.

[11] *Official Records,* 81

9th Vermont numbered around 450 men; of that number only 150 were experienced soldiers. Once the men were in line, Barney ordered that any of the new recruits who had yet to receive a musket and accouterments be issued them. Due to an insufficient supply of cartridge boxes, some of the new recruits were forced to carry their ammunition stuffed into their pockets.[12] Barney in describing the 9th Vermont to Colonel Jourdan would write that "our force there was small, and was composed nearly of new recruits you lately sent us, who had received their arms the same morning."[13]

After the new members of the 9th Vermont were provisioned Captain Kelley commenced running the command through drill. Many of the newly arrived soldiers had been in the United States Army for barely a month; some had yet to even learn the manual of arms for the operation of their newly issued muskets, and this would be their first introduction to the school of the soldier. With the Confederates undoubtedly heading towards their position officers

---

[12] *Wickman*, 279-280

[13] *Official Records*, 81

and veterans alike hoped the new men would be fast learners.[14]

As Captain Kelley was drilling the men of the 9th Vermont, Lieutenant Whitcher and the remainder of his party returned to Newport Barracks as instructed earlier in the day by Lieutenant Colonel Barney. Conspicuous by his absence was Captain Russell Conwell. Rather than return to Newport Barracks and his command, Conwell elected to proceed instead to the Union outpost at Croatan, fourteen miles away.

Once there the telegraph operator informed him that Newport Barracks was under attack. With this information, Conwell continued his journey to New Bern, where he would remain as the men under his command were left to fight the advancing Confederates.[15] With Conwell absent without leave, command of Company D of the 2nd Massachusetts Heavy Artillery fell to twenty-six year old Lieutenant John H. Foley, who before his service in that regiment had been wounded at the battles of Antietam and

---

[14] *Wickman*, 280.

[15] *Zeller*, 133.

Fredericksburg as a member of the 13th Massachusetts Infantry.[16]

With his orders from Colonel James Jourdan fresh in his mind, Lieutenant Colonel Valentine Barney elected to move towards the Bogue Sound Blockhouse with the infantry and cavalry under his command, leaving Lieutenant Foley and Company D of the 2nd Massachusetts Heavy Artillery at Newport Barracks to man the artillery there. By advancing forward Barney hoped he would run into Company B of the 9th Vermont, thus strengthening the regiment. Before marching out, Captain Samuel H. Kelley, in temporary command of the 9th Vermont, with the regimental colors in hand, addressed the men in the ranks with remarks that "reminded them of their duty as soldiers, and that the honor of their state was in their hands."[17]

After the brief speech, the men of the 9th Vermont and Companies A and B of the 23rd New York Cavalry marched in the direction of the

---

[16] Service Record of John H. Foley located at The National Archives in Washington, D.C.

[17] *Wickman*, 280

advancing Confederates, well aware that soon their force was to be engaged in battle with an enemy much greater in size than their small force.

Chapter Eight

"Fight As Long As Possible..."

February 2, 1864 had been a day of great success for Brigadier General Martin and his Confederates. With the capture and destruction of the Gales Creek and Bogue Sound blockhouses, the men in the ranks were flush with victory, but "the principal work of the day was still to be done.[1]" After regrouping his forces and burning the Bogue Sound Blockhouse, Martin and his command headed north along the County Road towards the Newport Barracks, four miles away. While there is no record of what time the Confederate left the Bogue Sound Blockhouse, it was likely after 1 p.m.

With orders from Colonel Jourdan to "fight as long as possible,[2]" Lieutenant Colonel Valentine Barney and the Union troops under his command began their advance south on the County Road, around 2 p.m., towards the Bogue Sound Blockhouse,

---

[1] *Wilmington Journal*, February 11, 1864

[2] *Official Records*, 78.

the very direction they heard the sounds of battle coming from just earlier in the day.[3]

The 9th Vermont "was halted about two miles from camp in a large clearing, extending across the County road and to the railroad track, which ran parallel to the road and half a mile from it.[4]" The cleaning was intermingled with marshes and was surrounded by open pine forests. Barney selected a location well suited for a smaller force to make a stand against a larger foe, as well as concealing their small numbers from the oncoming Confederates.[5]

The area where the Union line ran provided the advantage of cover from the wood lines, along with clear fields of fire in the direction of the advancing Confederates. The woods and marshes also gave some protection to the left and right flanks of the line. The County Road gave Barney and his men a reliable road to fall back on, if need be, towards Newport Barracks, in addition to being well suited for the placement of artillery in support of the infantry. With

---

3 *Zeller*, 134.

4 *Benedict*, 228.

5 *Wickman*, 280-281.

the decision of where to make his stand made, Barney deployed his troops.

That afternoon, Barney had 450 infantrymen, along with two companies of cavalry numbering around 150 troopers, to meet the advance of around 2,500 Confederates. The 9th Vermont was placed "in the edge of the woods in a thin single line – there being not men enough to form a line of battle for the front which must be covered – with skirmishers thrown out in the open ground in front.[6]" The skirmishers sent forward were divided into two wings by the County Road; the right wing under the command of 2nd Lieutenant Theodore Peck, of Company C, and the left wing under the command of 1st Lieutenant William Holman, of Company G.[7]

The far left of the skirmish line rested beyond the tracks of the Atlantic and North Carolina Railroad and continued across the County Road with the far right beside a marsh. Lieutenant Peck with part of his skirmishers was ordered "forward to ascertain the position of the enemy, and if possible, pen communication with Company B" that were thought

---

[6] *Benedict*, 228.

[7] *Zeller*, 134.

to be falling back to Newport Barracks down the County Road.[8] Peck and his detachment soon discovered a body of soldiers moving down the road, but to their dismay it was not their comrades from Company B.

Peck and his skirmishers advanced beyond a strip of woods and soon "came in sight of a strong body of the enemy's infantry, in process of forming a battle line.[9]" At almost the same moment, the Confederate line spotted the Union skirmishers and advanced towards them "firing heavily.[10]" Greatly outnumbered, Peck ordered his troops to fire one volley at the Confederates before falling back towards the main Union line. Along with Peck, Lieutenant Holman and the left wing of the Union skirmish line fell back to the main body of the 9th Vermont, posted at the edge of the wood line. As the skirmish line fell back Private James H. Grace, twenty-years old, was wounded in the head by a spent bullet as he bent down to pick up his ramrod. Falling

---

[8] *Benedict*, 228.

[9] Ibid.

[10] Ibid.

to the ground, Grace with the help of comrades, was helped to his feet and continued to fall back.[11]

Confederate accounts do not mention the initial skirmish with Peck and his detachment, but rather the fire of Union artillery. Brigadier General James Martin in his report states that after "advancing about 2 miles, as we emerged from a thick wood to a prairie and swamp the enemy opened on us with artillery.[12]" Another account written shortly after the battle described that "just as our forces were emerging from a dense wood into an open field, there were admonished by a shell from a six-pounder Parrott gun that the enemy were about to contest their further advance.[13]" This seems to suggest around the time Peck and his detachment fired on the advancing Confederates, Union artillery opened up as well. Understandably more attention was paid to the booming of artillery, as opposed to a handful of muskets. With this initial firing the Battle of Newport Barracks had now begun.

---

[11] *Zeller*, 134.

[12] *Official Records*, 85.

[13] *Wilmington Journal*, February 11, 1864

Encountering the fire of Union artillery and skirmishers, Martin prepared to deploy fully his command into a line of battle. In his report on the battle, Martin described the position of the Union line facing him and the deployment of his troops:

> He had formed line on rising ground, his front without trees, then a swamp, and then another unwooded field. In this second opening the Seventeenth and Forty-second formed line on the right and left of the road Colonel Jackson's infantry still father to the left, and the cavalry in reserve. Two companies from each regiment were thrown forward as skirmishers. The artillery was ordered to move forward on the road and use their guns as best they could.[14]

The four companies of Confederate skirmishers moved towards the main Union line and the familiar cracks of musketry began to ring out.

After establishing the extent of the Union line, Confederate skirmishers returned to their regiments and fell in with the rest of the infantry. The 17th North Carolina and the 42nd North Carolina now began the advance against the line of the undermanned 9th Vermont. The County Road split the two North

---

[14] *Official Records*, 85.

Carolina regiments as they advanced. Extending to the left of the County Road was the 42nd North Carolina commanded by Colonel John E. Brown, with the advance guard under Colonel George Jackson on their left flank. The 17th North Carolina commanded by Lieutenant Colonel John C. Lamb occupied a position to the right of the road. Occupying the road itself and in support of the infantry was Company A of the 3rd Battalion North Carolina Light Artillery under the command of Captain Andrew Ellis.

During the advance towards the position of the 9th Vermont, the right flank of the 17th North Carolina crossed the tracks of the Atlantic and North Carolina Railroad, effectively cutting off the Union defenders of Newport Barracks from Morehead City. Once in range, the 9th Vermont opened up with musket fire on the advancing North Carolinians. A Confederate soldier described the musket fire as "animated on both sides- rapid and continuous.[15]" As the infantry slugged it out for the next thirty minutes, the artillery on both sides dueled causing the ground to "quake with the deafening thunder, now filling the air with

---

[15] *Wilmington Journal*, February 11, 1864

the whizzing noise and loud screams of its shot and shell.[16]"

In the midst of the heavy fighting the Osier brothers of Company C of the 9th Vermont from Monkton, Vermont both became casualties. Private Joseph Osier was shot and killed instantly. Lieutenant Theodore Peck standing close by witnessed the scene. He described Private Osier as "a fine looking fellow only 18-years-old, and a new recruit. He died fighting bravely.[17]"

Older brother, Private Peter Osier, nineteen-years old, was later wounded in the fighting that day. Peter Osier unable to keep up with the rest of the regiment was captured, and held in a Confederate prison. Private Peter Osier would die of his wounds only a few days after being exchanged. Both Osier brothers are buried in United States National Cemeteries; Joseph in New Bern, North Carolina and Peter in Annapolis, Maryland.[18]

---

[16] *The Carolina Watchman Weekly*, Salisbury, North Carolina. February 22, 1864.

[17] *Zeller*, 135

[18] Ibid.

With the fighting increasing in intensity, Brigadier General Martin, riding directly behind his men, ordered his infantry to charge the Union lines and dislodge the 9th Vermont from the position that for the last half-hour they had defended doggedly.[19] The 17th and 42nd North Carolina charged enthusiastically forward; one North Carolina soldier described that "every gun was loaded, every bayonet fixed, and every heart filled with patriotic devotion to his Sunny South.[20]"

The renewed Confederate push was too much for the 9th Vermont to hold back. Sergeant Charles Branch of the 9th Vermont would write that "our line was compelled to give way and falling back a short distance a new line was formed which after a continuation of the firing was again charged and forced to fall back.[21]"

For the next two hours the fighting at Newport Barracks would see the 9th Vermont make stand after stand, only to be forced from each position by the larger 17th and 42nd North Carolina regiments.

---

[19] *Official Records*, 85.

[20] *Carolina Watchman*, February 22, 1864

[21] *Wickman*, 282.

Despite falling back, the men from Vermont made the attacking North Carolinians fight hard for every inch of ground gained.

One member of the 9th Vermont noted that the men in the ranks maintained "good order, loading and delivering their fire, as they retreated, with great coolness, and with marked effect upon the enemy.[22]" Even with the odds clearly against them the men of the 9th Vermont continued to fight on desperately, with the help from one officer, a few men, and a single artillery piece.

Lieutenant Eugene Viele of the 9th Vermont and a group of men from Company D of the 2nd Massachusetts Heavy Artillery "manned a field-piece, drawing it out from the camp by hand. Stationing this in the road, he opened fire on the enemy's artillery, exploded one of their caissons, and by repeated discharges of grape aided in checking the Confederate advance.[23]" Viele and his make-shift gun crew "played

---

[22] *Wickman*, 282.

[23] *Benedict*, 229. The "grape" mentioned was a type of artillery round known as grapeshot. It was often used against infantry attacks by showering the oncoming troops with nine iron or lead balls. The writer could also be referring to canister, similar to

havoc in the ranks of the rebs.[24]" That afternoon, the Union troops defending Newport Barracks could use all the help they could get; and Viele and his gunners provided valuable service in support of the pressed infantrymen of the 9th Vermont.

The 9th Vermont received further support between 3 p.m. and 4 p.m. when what remained of Company H, engaged that morning at the Gales Creek Blockhouse, joined the rest of the regiment. Captain Gorman formed his small company and joined the rest of the 9th Vermont on the firing line, as one soldier put it, just in "time to join in the melee.[25]" Despite the additional men in the ranks and a valiant defense, the men of the 9th Vermont was pushed back ever closer to Newport Barracks. As Company C of the 9th Vermont fell back, Lieutenant James F. Bolton was wounded and had to be carried from the field.[26] Bolton was not the only officer to become a casualty in this portion of the fight. Lieutenant William C.

---

grapeshot, but more common at the time of the Civil War. Canister used twenty-seven iron or lead balls.

[24] *Wickman,* 282

[25] Ibid.

[26] *Zeller*, 134

Holden was captured with a number of his men as they fell back to a new position.[27] The loss of experienced officers was a serious blow to a regiment composed mostly of inexperienced troops.

By 5:30 p.m., Lieutenant Colonel Barney, after making ten separate stands, ordered the color guard of the 9th Vermont to place the regimental colors on the crest of a low hill overlooking Newport Barracks. This is where the eleventh and final stand of the day was made.[28] The 9th Vermont over the course of three hours was pushed back almost two miles from their initial position. Barney knew, as was the case with the previous ten positions, all the 9th Vermont could do atop the crest of the hill was slow the North Carolinians. It was hoped this stand could buy enough time for the command to fall back to Newport Barracks, where the artillery and earthworks would give the beleaguered regiment a fighting chance to defend their post. Unfortunately for the 9th Vermont this stand at Newport Barracks was not to be.

During the confusion of the fighting that afternoon, the men of Company D of the 2nd

---

[27] *Official Records*, 81.

[28] *Wickman*, 285.

Massachusetts Heavy Artillery had inexplicitly spiked the artillery at Newport Barracks, rendering the guns useless. After falling across the Newport River over the County Road Bridge, the men of Company D also spiked the 32-pounder, located at a redoubt on the outskirts of Shepardsville.[29]

It has been speculated that had the men of Company D of the 2nd Massachusetts Heavy Artillery stayed at their guns that a stand by the infantry might have been made.[30] A Confederate soldier writing a few weeks after the battle discussed such a possibility stating that "if they had fallen back to their stronghold and made a firm stand, the probability is we would have been very materially; but such a course their unparalleled cowardice would not allow them even to think of.[31]"

With no artillery support to keep the overwhelming Confederate numbers back, the use of the earthworks at Newport Barracks was now out of the question and the fighting at Newport Barracks

---

[29] *Benedict*, 229.

[30] Ibid.

[31] *Carolina Watchman*, February 22, 1864

now reached a critical point for the men of the 9th Vermont. With both routes to Morehead City cut off by the infantry of the 17th and 42nd North Carolina, Lieutenant Colonel Valentine Barney turned his focus from defending Newport Barracks to saving his entire command from capture.

The 9th Vermont formed for the eleventh and final time that day on the low crest in front of Newport Barracks with its ranks thinned from casualties. Barney ordered a detail to set fire to the barracks, hospital, and military stores at Newport Barracks to prevent them from falling into the hands of Confederate forces. As a dark smoke began to rise from Newport Barracks, the 9th Vermont fired one last volley before moving quickly across the Newport River over the railroad trestle and the County Road Bridge.[32]

To cover the withdrawal of the regiment over the bridges, Barney sent Adjutant Josiah O. Livingston with orders to Lieutenants Theodore Peck and Erastus Jewett to hold the two bridges until the entire command crossed. After the 9th Vermont was across, both officers were to set both structures on

---

[32] *Benedict*, 230

fire, putting the Newport River between them and the Southern troops. Adjutant Livingston passed along the order from Lieutenant Colonel Barney to both Peck and Jewett that "the bridges must be burned at all hazards."[33]

Lieutenant Jewett and the men of his rear guard crossed to the north side of the Newport River and took position just on the other side of the railroad trestle. Jewett later wrote:

> We held the bridge and twice drove the enemy back to the cover of the woods. They then shelled us with a battery at about 600 yards, for fifteen minutes, but as soon as they stopped, we were at them again with our muskets, and succeeded in keeping them back from the bridge till it was burned, so they could not cross the river.[34]

The Confederate battery mentioned was most likely that of Captain Andrew Paris and the Staunton Hill Artillery from Virginia. This battery was held in reserve for most of the battle, until ordered up to shell the Union defenders of the railroad trestle.

---

33 *Zeller*, 138.

34 Ibid. 139.

In an attempt to carry the trestle, elements of the 17th North Carolina deployed as skirmishers and twice were "kept back by a vigorous fire of musketry" from Jewett and his men.[35] It was during this fire fight that Captain James J. Leith, a thirty-six year old farmer from Hyde County, from Company B of the 17th North Carolina was mortally wounded "leading his men into the hottest of the fire."[36] Brigadier James Martin would describe Leith as "a brave and efficient officer."[37] Despite the efforts of Leith and the men from the 17th North Carolina, Adjutant Josiah Livingston was able to successfully set the trestle on fire.

As Jewett and Livingston were completing their orders at the railroad trestle, Lieutenant Theodore Peck and his men of his rear guard were pressed strongly by the 42nd North Carolina near the County Road Bridge. Peck was earlier told to expect cavalry with turpentine and tar on the other side of the Newport River, but as he reached the County Road

---

35 *Benedict*, 230

36 *Carolina Watchman*, March 7, 1864.

37 *Official Records*, 86

Bridge; neither the cavalry nor the turpentine or tar was to be found and Peck was forced to improvise.[38]

Taking a handful of men while the rest of the rear guard held off the 42nd North Carolina, Peck and the men began to tear up loose planks on the wooden bridge and with dry grass as kindling were able to set the structure on fire.[39] Peck, along with the rear guard, soon crossed the bridge and continued to fire at the 42nd North Carolina. It was at this time that Martin ordered Captain Ellis with his battery to fire canister at the remaining members of the 9th Vermont on the opposite bank in a last ditch effort to capture the bridge.[40]

As the fight between the last rear guard of the 9th Vermont and the 42nd North Carolina was reaching its height, Peck was told that Sergeant Charles Branch of Company A of the 9th Vermont was unable to get across the bridge after suffering a concussion from a Confederate artillery round. Peck soon rushed across the burning bridge under a hail of lead to help Branch across. Back across the bridge again with Branch, the

---

[38] *Zeller*, 138

[39] *Benedict*, 230

[40] *Zeller*, 139

County Road Bridge, weakened by the heat and flames collapsed into the Newport River. With their task complete, Peck and his men marched to rejoin the rest of the 9th Vermont on the outskirts of Shepardsville.[41]

With the bridges destroyed and the Newport River between the Confederates and his command, Lieutenant Colonel Barney issued one last order to Captain Linus Sherman and the provost guard to burn the government stores of turpentine in the village of Shepardsville. Once completed, what was left of the Newport Barracks garrison began their twenty-three mile march through swamps and around the inlets to Beaufort.[42]

Brigadier General James Martin and his Confederate forces were now in control of Newport Barracks after a sharp and hard fought battle against the Union defenders. As they entered the barracks their attention was drawn to the United States garrison flag flying above the post. A soldier in the ranks wrote shortly after the battle what happened next:

---

[41] Ibid.

[42] Ibid.

Over the deserted stronghold waved that emblem of oppression the "Stars and Stripes." This was soon hauled down. Reader, you know the fate of a slice of bloody meat when thrown to a pack of starving wolves. A similar one this detested flag met with. It was trampled in the dust and torn into a thousand fragments.[43]

As the men of Martin's command celebrated their third conquest of the day, the sun began to set over the area. It was now a little after 6 p.m. and the growing darkness brought an end to the Battle of Newport Barracks.

---

43 *Carolina Watchman*, February 22, 1864

Chapter Nine

"One of the greatest panics..."

As the 9th Vermont and the rest of the garrison of Newport Barracks retreated to Beaufort, Brigadier James Martin and his Confederates were basking in the hard earned glow of victory. Just shy of two years later, Southern forces had reclaimed Shepardsville, which had been under Union occupation since March 21, 1862. With the occupation of Newport Barracks, the victorious Confederates began to collect any of the remaining Union stores and gear that remained behind from the garrison's retreat.

In the wake of the Union retreat many of the buildings at Newport Barracks were set on fire in order to prevent their capture by Confederate troops. As the men of the 17th and 42nd North Carolina pushed over the earthworks in pursuit of the retreating 9th Vermont, many broke ranks in an attempt to put out the fires that were raging in an attempt to salvage any stores or supplies that could be saved from the flames.

One soldier would write that "the fruits of our victory were as follows: quantities of commissary, quartermaster, and ordinance stores, all sorts of camp and garrison equipage, a large number of small arms, eight pieces of artillery, and ninety prisoners.[1]" For Confederate soldiers, already feeling the shortages of food and equipment, any captured Union food or supplies were a welcome sight.

As night settled over Newport Barracks, Brigadier General Martin ordered a well deserved rest for his men. In his report, Martin stated that "the fire on the railroad bridge was extinguished, but later in the evening I judged it best to burn it. It was now too dark to follow the enemy.[2]" Despite not capturing the garrison of Newport Barracks, the day was still a smashing success for Martin and his troops. After the battle, Martin wrote:

> The results of the expedition are 4 heavy dirt forts captured, 3 block-houses, with 1 flag, 10 pieces of artillery, 20 barrels of powder, several hundred small-arms, 200 boxes fixed ammunition for artillery, a considerable quantity of forage and other stores, 1,000 barrels of turpentine belonging to the United States, the quarters, stables, and store-houses, called Newport Barracks, for 1,000 infantry, two companies of cavalry, and one

---

[1] *Carolina Watchman*, February 22, 1864.

[2] *Official Records*, 85

of artillery; 3 railroad bridges, some trestle-work, some of the track at Croatan, and 2 large county bridges, all burnt of destroyed expect for one piece of artillery brought away. About 30 horses and 2 wagons were brought off and the telegraph wire was cut. The men saved from the burning buildings many overcoats, blankets, and other articles of clothing.[3]

The victory at Newport Barracks was a memorable experience for many of the men in Southern ranks that day. While an impressive and hard earned victory, many of the soldiers focused less on the fighting they had endured, and more on the captured Union goods. W.H. Wyatt of Company H of the 17th North Carolina in a post war memoir recounted that "our brass band came back togged out in brand new U.S. Infantry uniforms. All agreed that the United States troops were well supplied with good food, of which fact they had the most convincing and agreeable proof.[4]"

---

3 *Official Records*, 86. The additional blockhouse and railroad bridges were from the scouting operation that Martin ordered on February 3, 1864.

4 *Wyatt*, 18.

A soldier and amateur newspaper correspondent from the 42nd North Carolina went into even more detail:

> The Yankees had time to fire their commissary store houses most effectually before their departure- But fortunately, they did not have time to carry off their knapsacks, and our brave men captured clothing in vast quantities.
>
> Overcoats, pants, caps, vests, shoes, boots, blacking, coffee, sugar, tea, rice, potatoes, beans, onions and a hundred other things too numerous to mention, were the spoils of victory.
>
> Your correspondent feasted that night on the following bill of fare: Tea, Coffee, and White Sugar, Ham and Eggs, Strawberry Preserves and Biscuit, Mountain Butter and Crackers! Beat it yea can, ye fifteen dollar-a day Hotel! And who wouldn't be a solider![5]

Another soldier recounted to *The Wilmington Journal* that:

> It was now night, and after a running fight of six hours, over the distance of eight miles, our gallant troops were in possession of the field- the enemy flying for life. Altogether, our troops captured seven pieces of artillery, several hundred stand of arms, two hundred boxes of ammunition, about seventy-five prisoners, six slaves, a dozen horses, and commissary stores

---

[5] *Carolina Watchman*, March 7, 1864

enough to subsist the troops during their stay in the neighborhood, besides a large quantity of clothing with which our men supplied themselves- such as overcoats, pants, blankets, &c. The enemy burnt most of their quartermaster and commissary stores. They also burnt their stables with the horses in them. Some few horses were rescued by our men. In addition to our captures, we destroyed one thousand barrels of turpentine belonging to the U.S. government and burnt two bridges.[6]

First Lieutenant Augustus Leazer, twenty-years old at the time of the battle, of Company G of the 42nd North Carolina, recounted to his daughter after the war that he found a sword and "a volume of Blackstone now in our library, inscribed with the name of "John M. Laughlin, 1st Lieut. Co. A., 103 Penna. Regiment, Penna. Vols.[7]" Lieutenant Leazer, remembering the lack of coffee on the Confederate home front, sent home to his mother in Rowan

---

[6] *The Wilmington Journal*, February 11, 1864

[7] Carry A. Leazer, *Sketch of Confederate Service of Lieutenant Augustus Leazer, Co. G 42d Regt. N.C. State troops, March 1862-May 2, 1865.* North Carolina State Archives in Raleigh. The 103rd Pennsylvania was not at Newport Barracks, but did serve in New Bern. It is likely this book was borrowed by a member of the Newport Barracks garrison and unfortunately left behind before it could be returned to its owner Lieutenant John M. Laughlin of the 103rd Pennsylvania.

County a sack of coffee. The coffee was a welcome gift to his mother who "was roasting rye and chipped sweet potatoes at home" as a substitute due to the scarcity of coffee during the war.[8]

As the Confederates who occupied Newport Barracks relished their victory, the men of the 9th Vermont and the Newport Barracks garrison were making "its way in the gathering darkness, by a long detour around the swamps and inlet, to Beaufort, where it arrived at sunrise next morning.[9]" While Beaufort was only 15 miles distant via the rail line and a ship across the sound, the detour that the 9th Vermont took was closer to 27 miles though very difficult terrain. Captain Linus Sherman of the 9th Vermont described his experiences that night:

> I started on horseback & rode 5 or 6 miles & found a man shot through the foot. I let him ride and the scamp rode on and I have not seen him since. During the march the wagon master kindly offered to let me ride & I rode a few miles more.[10]

---

[8] Ibid.

[9] *Benedict*, 230

[10] *Zeller*, 139

Private Benjamin Stokes of Company C of the 9th Vermont was severely injured after tripping over a fallen tree on the retreat; the effects of the injury later caused him to receive a disability pension after the war.[11]

After a night spent trudging through bone chilling swamps with very little gear the men of the 9th Vermont entered Beaufort early in the morning of February 3. The men of the 9th Vermont after the march were described as "hungry, faint and exhausted by a forced night march of twenty-seven miles.[12]" A member of Company H of the 9th Vermont described the experience as "the most I can say is, we have had a severe time and have suffered considerably.[13]"

Private Lyman Chamberlain, a hospital steward in Beaufort, described in great detail the appearance of the Newport Barracks garrison as they entered Beaufort:

> Wednesday morning just at day break the largest part of the retreating force came into this village. They were nearly all tired out and looking most mighty tough. Some barefoot and

---

[11] Ibid.

[12] *Benedict*, 230

[13] *Wickman*, 289

others covered with mud from head to foot. Most of them had thrown away their knapsacks, guns, and equipments.[14]

Private Chamberlain continued:

> Soon as they came in we commenced here at the hospital to prepare them a breakfast which was done at short notice. It was eat at a short notice for they were all very hungry both officers and men for they had run all night.[15]

After breakfast and a short rest, the 9th Vermont was ferried across the inlet to Morehead City to help augment the scant forces thrown together in the defense of the town from the expected Confederate attack. Once across and on the ground the 9th Vermont had a welcome sight waiting for them: Company B of that regiment who had retreated from the Bogue Sound Blockhouse to Morehead City. When they were reunited with their comrades they found "all hands were set actively at work digging

---

[14] *Chamberlain,* Letter Seventeen

[15] Ibid.

rifle-pits, in anticipation of an attack from Martin's force.[16]"

The appearance of Martin's Confederate force and the subsequent capture of Newport Barracks caused what was described as "one of the greatest panics that has happened during the war" in Morehead City and Beaufort.[17] On February 3, James Rumley in Beaufort wrote in his diary that:

> Supposing the Confederates intend to march upon Beaufort, the Yankee commandant here, Capt. Fuller, who has been sent here with his company from Fort Macon, has erected barricades of sawed lumber and pine wood on Front and Market Streets and is planting cannon to defend the place. Some of the Yankee traders and terrified negroes are packing up their movables, intending to seek safety on board of vessels under the guns of Fort Macon. The Negro schools are suspended, and the teachers, male and female, are evidently preparing to slink off.[18]

---

[16] *Benedict*, 232

[17] Judkin Browning and Michael Thomas Smith, editors. *Letters from a North Carolina Unionist* (Raleigh, North Carolina: Division of Archives and History, 2001) 181.

[18] *Southern Mind*, 123

Rumley, a Southern sympathizer, continued that "it does the heart good to see these intruders upon our soil, and violators of our laws, quailing before the sound of Confederate cannon, and trembling at the approach of the power which they have long insulted and defied.[19]"

Private Lyman Chamberlain described further Beaufort during the panic:

> As our men retreated to this place, it was of course expected that the rebel force would follow them and so it raised considerable excitement in this village as well as at the hospital. For in the village there was a large quantity of government stores and officer's wives and children, and at the hospital sick men and medical supplies. Which of course must be saved at all risks so all of the Government stores or nearly all were loaded on the boats and shoved off into the stream and anchored under the guns of Fort Macon. Every citizen and negro in the place for a mile around were forced to take and axe or shovel and build entrenchments around the place. At the hospital every man that was able to leave his bed had to take his gun and ammunition and be ready at a minutes warning supposing an attack was made.[20]

---

[19] Ibid.

[20] *Chamberlain*, Letter Seventeen

Mary von Olnhausen, an army nurse in Morehead City, wrote in a letter a few days after the battle the scene in that town:

Soon the negroes began to flock in; they came by hundreds, such frightened beings, leaving everything except their children behind them. The gunboats (one I mean, a small one) came up and lay opposite the town. Every citizen was compelled to take arms, and every negro was put to work on the entrenchments.

Such a scurrying time you never saw. All the company stores were sent on board ships, and all the stores of the regiment too; and everyone began to pack his traps.[21]

Von Olnhausen, described the night of February 2 in great detail:

By dark we could see Newport Barracks burning, but you could learn nothing of the men who defended it. You never did hear of such a night, I guess as that was- the citizen women screaming from every house, so loud that we could hear them, because their men were compelled to fight and, of course, be killed without mercy; the terrified negroes constantly arriving; the thousand reports brought in each moment; the occasional

[21] *Adventures of an Army Nurse*, 133

firing of a gun by some very scared sentry; and always such a rushing to and fro.[22]

At Newport Barracks on February 3, Brigadier General James Martin anxiously awaited word from New Bern from Major General George Pickett. In the meantime, Martin ordered his men to conduct reconnaissance in the area around Newport Barracks. Martin described the following in his report on the battle:

> A detachment of cavalry, under Colonel Jackson, was sent toward Morehead City early on the morning of the 3d, and another, under Lieutenant Colonel Jeffords, toward New Berne. Small ones were also sent on other roads. On the return of Colonel Jackson he reported the road so blocked up by trees as to be impassable to cavalry. An infantry party was then ordered to Morehead City but was recalled on account of General Barton's dispatches.
>
> Lieutenant Colonel Jeffords made his reconnaissance to within 1 ½ miles of New Berne with an energy and soundness of judgment worthy of high commendation.[23]

---

[22] Ibid.

[23] *Official Records*, 86

During most of his time at Newport Barracks, Brigadier General Martin was trying his best to ascertain exactly what was going on in New Bern. Writing to General Whiting in Wilmington at 8 p.m. on February 2, he expressed his desire to continue on to Morehead City, as well as his frustrations with the lack of word from New Bern:

> There are now only a few organized commands on this point of land between Newport River and the sound. I shall send early in the morning to Morehead City and occupy it. I am very much embarrassed to know what to do on account of my entire ignorance of the state of affairs at New Berne. I have heard from General Barton only once, of which I wrote to you before.[24]

Shortly after his dispatch to Whiting, Martin sent a dispatch at 9:30 p.m. to General Seth Barton or any Confederate commander around New Bern who could assist him:

> We drove the enemy from this place just at dusk this evening. I am at a loss to know what to do now, as I have heard nothing from you or from New Berne. In this state of my information I deem it best to burn the railroad bridge. Please ask General Lee or General Pickett to give me some instructions at

---

[24] Ibid. 88

once. You know my rear is exposed to an attack from New Berne the moment you leave it open. Please let me hear from you or the general in command of the forces around New Berne.[25]

It is interesting to note the mention of General Robert E. Lee in the dispatch. While Lee was not in command in New Bern, rumor of such must have been making the rounds among Confederate forces before and during the operation.

At 2:30 a.m. on February 3, a dispatch from General Seth Barton at New Bern finally reached Martin:

My part of the expedition has failed; has accomplished very little, and I now leave to join the main body. There is, therefore, no force between you and New Berne.[26]

Around 4:30 a.m. another dispatch from Barton reached Newport Barracks directing Martin to hold his command at that point. On receiving this, Martin sent a return dispatch back:

I have received your dispatch telling me General Pickett wishes me to cut and hold the railroad. I informed you by

---

[25] Ibid.

[26] Ibid.

> courier last night that I have burnt the railroad bridge. I should have left this morning on my return but for your last dispatch. My situation here is very precarious if the enemy should throw re-enforcements into Morehead City. I have sent out scouting parties in every direction this morning. From my information I am hardly able to take Morehead City, and a failure would injure me more than not making the attempt. Please keep me informed at least once a day of the state of affairs.[27]

It is not clear as to exactly why Martin felt he could not capture Morehead City. At the time the town was lightly defended by a skeleton force hastily thrown together. The best possible explanation is that Martin was afraid to commit his forces into action at Morehead City with his rear open to a counterattack from New Bern.

With his command ultimately unsuccessful in their attack on New Bern, Major General George Pickett ordered his commanders to break off any attacks and withdraw. At 6:30 p.m. on February 3, Martin received a short dispatch from Barton that stated "Fall back. All the troops are withdrawn. I do not know what it means.[28]" With that dispatch,

---

[27] Ibid. 89

[28] Ibid.

Martin prepared to withdraw his command from Newport Barracks and back to Wilmington the next day. Martin wrote that "about 8 o'clock on the morning of the 4th instant we left Newport Barracks on our return.[29]" Martin and his Confederates returned to Wilmington on February 10.

On February 5, Colonel Edward Ripley arrived from Fort Monroe and resumed command of the 9th Vermont. That day the 9th Vermont and the 21st Connecticut infantry along with one piece of artillery, under the overall command of Colonel James Jourdan, advanced towards Newport Barracks. Jourdan and his Union troops arrived at Newport Barracks around 6 p.m.

Finding the post abandoned by the Confederates, Jourdan ordered the 23rd New York Cavalry, under Captain Cummings, to scout the area and discover the location of Martin and his Confederate force. On February 6, Captain Cummings returned to Newport Barracks and

---

[29] Ibid. 86

informed Jourdan that he spotted the campfires of the Confederates about 11 miles away.[30]

On the afternoon of February 6, the Union forces at Newport Barracks received a report that part of the Confederate cavalry of Martin's command was 5 miles from their location. The 23rd New York Cavalry was called upon to investigate this report and found it to be accurate.

With the discovery the 23rd New York Cavalry charged forward and drove the Confederates back towards their camp. At the Confederate camp were 350 cavalry under Colonel Jeffords, who with the support of artillery forced the men of the 23rd New York Cavalry to withdraw back to Newport Barracks. According the report of Colonel James Jourdan, the losses suffered by the 23rd New York Cavalry totaled two horses captured. It was also reported that they recovered five wounded soldiers and brought them back to Newport Barracks.[31]

After the skirmish with the Confederate cavalry of Martin's rear guard, Jourdan and his men began to strengthen the area around Newport Barracks for the

---

[30] Ibid. 79

[31] Ibid.

defense. On February 7, a rumor of an impending Confederate attack forced the Union troops at Newport Barracks to fall back again from the position. The rumor turned out to be false and by February 8, Union forces once again occupied Newport Barracks.[32]

On February 9, Colonel James Jourdan led another reconnaissance in force, towards Cedar Point and the White Oak River. His force consisted of the 9th Vermont, 21st Connecticut, and the 158th New York infantry, with a section of artillery. When the force reached Peletier's Mills, they learned that Martin and his Confederates had crossed over the White Oak River and was once again in Onslow County. With the information that there was no longer any Confederate forces in his front to threaten his lines, Jourdan and his men returned. Two wounded Confederates left behind by Martin and his retreating forces were captured. One of the horses captured by Confederates just a few days earlier was also recovered.[33]

---

32 Ibid.

33 Ibid. 79-80

With the Confederate threat receding with every mile closer to Wilmington that Martin and his troops marched, the period of panic and anxiety was now over. The men of the 9th Vermont once again occupied Newport Barracks and reestablished their outposts at Bogue Sound, Canady's Mills, and Gales Creek. After over a week of great excitement, life at Newport Barracks returned to the routine it had known before Martin's attack.[34]

[34] *Zeller*, 141

Epilogue

The Cost and Legacy of the Battle of Newport Barracks, February 2, 1864

The Battle of Newport Barracks was a great Confederate tactical victory overshadowed by a great Confederate strategic loss. In his report, Major General W.H.C Whiting in forwarding the after action report of Brigadier General James Martin to Confederate Adjutant and Inspector General Samuel Cooper in Richmond, Virginia stated that:

> General Martin and his force fully accomplished their object and deserve much credit for gallant and skillful conduct. In my opinion he could have prevented re-enforcements from reaching the enemy by way of the Neuse.[1]

Martin in closing his report heaped praise on the soldiers under his command in the battle:

> I cannot close this report without expressing my gratification at the gallant behavior of the troops during the fight

---

[1] *Official Records*, 84

and the patient endurance on the march of nearly 240 miles over very heavy roads.[2]

The contemporary press coverage was nothing but positive for the role Martin and his Confederate force played in the Battle of Newport Barracks, and the operation as a whole. *The Wilmington Journal* on February 11, 1864 was highly complimentary of the performance of Martin and his command at Newport Barracks:

> It will be seen that General Martin, with the gallant officers and men under his command, accomplished all and more than had been assigned to them, and if blame attached anywhere for the comparative failure of the combined movements, none of that blame can attach to General Martin or the brave little army under his command.[3]

The Carolina Watchman in Salisbury, North Carolina carried the account of a soldier from the 42nd North Carolina that stated:

> A more successful expedition than ours, in every respect, has never been planned. With a loss of twenty men killed and wounded, we have inflicted a loss upon the enemy of at least five

---

[2] Ibid. 86

[3] *The Wilmington Journal*, February 11, 1864.

times that number in killed and wounded, besides about seventy five prisoners. We have damaged him to a large amount of supplies, and in munitions of war, and finally, we have convinced him, that he holds his boasted territory, in North Carolina by a very precarious tenure.[4]

While the writer in his account exaggerated the number of Union casualties quite a bit, the sentiment and pride he and his fellow soldiers felt about the operation were clear.

For their Union counterparts, while they had put up a valiant defense, it was still a defeat that was tough to swallow. One post-war account sums up the feelings many had after the battle:

The feelings of the officers and men of the command, as they halted and dropped in their tracks at Beaufort, may be imagined. They had been driven from their camp, saving nothing but their arms and the clothing on their backs. They were hungry, faint and exhausted by a forced night march of twenty-seven miles. They missed comrades from their number, who were killed, drowned or in the enemy's hands. Yet they had done some fighting; and, considering that half their number were raw recruits, many of whom had never handled a musket, and that they had held their ground for hours against greatly superior

---

[4] *Carolina Watchman*, March 7, 1864

numbers, they thought they had done pretty well. They had at least frustrated a well-laid plan for their capture. They had their colors and their arms, and the right to use them. So it might have been worse.[5]

Lieutenant Colonel Barney, writing to his wife three days after the battle from Morehead City, expressed his feelings on the performance of his men in the recent battle:

> Our new recruits composed nearly all of our force having but about 60, or 70, of the old men present- The recruits had guns put in their hands about 3 or 4 hours before the fight- and hardly any of them how to right face but they fought finely considering the circumstances.[6]

In his official report, Barney echoed his earlier sentiments when he wrote "I am assured that the Ninth Vermont has done itself great credit in the late engagement.[7]" Colonel James Jourdan likewise commended the 9th Vermont for their performance in the battle in his report stating the men held their position and it "was not until there was great danger

---

[5] *Benedict*, 230
[6] Jeffery D. Marshall, editor. *A War of the People: Vermont Civil War Letters* (Hanover, New Hampshire: University Press of New England, 1999.) 207.
[7] *Official Records*, 82

of all retreat being cut off that the order to abandon the place was given.[8]" Colonel Edward Ripley of the 9th Vermont applauded his men during the battle writing that "the conduct of the Regt was without exception calculated to make all its friends proud of it.[9]"

Any concern that Lieutenant Colonel Valentine Barney had over his performance in the battle was put to rest with a conversation he had with Colonel James Jourdan. Barney would write to his wife that "I have been told by Col. Jourdan Comdg this district that I had done the very best that possibly could be so I feel that I have not been disgraced even if I was obliged to destroy everything and retreat.[10]"

The 23rd New York Cavalry were commended by Colonel Jourdan for their role in the battle:

> The two companies, Mix's new cavalry, did good service and were continually harassing the enemy at different points. Lieutenant Budlong deserves special mention for this bravery upon several occasions.[11]

---

[8] Ibid. 77
[9] *Wickman*, 294
[10] Ibid. 295
[11] *Official Records*, 77

Jourdan, while praising the performance of the 9th Vermont and 23rd New York Cavalry, was equally harsh in his assessment of the actions of Company D of the 2nd Massachusetts Heavy Artillery. Jourdan in his report wrote:

> Company D, Second Massachusetts Heavy Artillery, garrisoning the fort at Newport Barracks, rendered but little assistance as a company, having failed to properly work their guns; a few, however, joined the Ninth Vermont and manned a gun under Lieutenant Viele, of the Ninth. This probably was owing to the absence of their commanding officer, Captain Conwell, who left his command on the morning of the 2d and never returned, and to the inexperience of the lieutenants in charge.[12]

Overall the Union defenders of Newport Barracks fought bravely in the face of overwhelming odds, only retiring from the field to prevent their capture. Their Confederate adversaries displayed equal courage and tenacity in their victories at Gales Creek and Bogue Sound Blockhouses and Newport Barracks. Other than the Company D of the 2nd Massachusetts Heavy Artillery, it could be said all the men who struggled and sacrificed on February 2, 1864

---

[12] Ibid.

did not only their commands proud, but also the states from which they hailed.

As with any battle there is always a human cost, and the Battle of Newport Barracks is no different. Brigadier General James Martin in his official report placed losses of his Confederate forces at 6 killed and 14 wounded.[13] Lieutenant Colonel Valentine Barney, commander of the Union forces, placed his loss at 3 killed, 13 wounded, and 51 captured.[14]

An exhaustive examination of the Service Records for each command that fought at Newport Barracks, found some differences in totals from the official casualty reports.

Martin's account of 6 killed is correct, only 5 known wounded have been found. Most likely the true number of wounded is a bit higher than that Martin's report (in the 20 to 25 range), based on Union accounts of Confederate wounded. While Martin does not report any of his men missing or captured, contemporary civilian and military accounts

---

[13] *Official Records*, 86
[14] Ibid. 81

do point to a handful of Confederates who were wounded and captured.

Barney in his report stated 3 killed, with the examination of the service records showing 5 killed. His report for wounded matches almost perfectly with the numbers gleaned from the service records with Barney claiming 13 wounded, only off by 1 from the 14 found. The same is true for the reports of Union captured with 51 reported, with 49 found. Barney did not include the numbers for the other units of his command that day.

The Service Records of the 23rd New York Cavalry and Company D of the 2nd Massachusetts Heavy Artillery show 10 captured for the former and 5 for the latter.

A somber note is that of the 64 Union soldiers who became casualties that day, 39 (61%) would eventually die in captivity in Confederate prisons.

It is likely we will never know the exact total of casualties at the Battle of Newport Barracks; the known casualties from both sides are 11 killed, 19 wounded, and 64 captured for total of 94.

The Union dead were sent back to their homes in Vermont or were buried in the National Cemetery in New Bern, North Carolina. The Confederates killed at Newport Barracks seem to have been buried at that location. An account shortly after the battle states that "on account of a great lack of transportation, we were compelled to inter our dead upon the same field where they fought and displayed so much gallantry and heroism.[15]"

After the Battle of Newport Barracks, the Civil War raged for over a year before it finally ended. The Confederate units at Newport Barracks continued to fight until the bitter end of the war before ultimately surrendering.

The 17th and 42nd North Carolina would go on to fight in Virginia, taking part in the Bermuda Hundred Campaign, Cold Harbor, and Petersburg. Eventually they would head back to North Carolina, fighting around Wilmington, before surrendering at Greensboro in May of 1865.

Company E of the 5th North Carolina Cavalry and Company K of the 5th South Carolina Cavalry

---

[15] *Carolina Watchman*, February 22, 1864

joined the Army of Northern Virginia fighting for a time under famous Confederates J.E.B. Stuart and Wade Hampton. They remained with that army until the surrender at Appomattox in April of 1865.

The artillery of Martin's Confederate force, Company A of the 3rd North Carolina Battalion Light Artillery and the Staunton Hill (Virginia) Artillery remained in Wilmington and took part in the battles around that city in January and February of 1865.

The Union forces at Newport Barracks, while defeated at that battle, would serve on until the Union victory in the Civil War. While the 23rd New York Cavalry and Company D of the 2nd Massachusetts Heavy Artillery continued to serve in North Carolina until being mustered out in July of 1865, the 9th Vermont were sent back to Virginia a few months after the battle.

The 9th Vermont fought in the Bermuda Hundred Campaign and later with much distinction at the Battle of Fort Harrison outside of Richmond. For a hard luck regiment like the 9th Vermont, after surrendering at Harper's Ferry and retreating at Newport Barracks, there was a great sense of pride when the regiment was one of the first to enter the Confederate capital of Richmond after it had been evacuated by the retreating Southern forces heading west, eventually to Appomattox.

With the war ending, the men who fought at Newport Barracks and survived went home to continue or, in some cases, rebuild their lives. Most of the veterans of Newport Barracks simply lived their lives quietly after the war, but some gained some measure of fame or notoriety.

Captain Russell Conwell, of Company D of the 2nd Massachusetts Heavy Artillery, was tried by an Army Court Martial and was stripped of his command and rank for abandoning his command without orders. Conwell appealed his case all the way up to President Abraham Lincoln, before finally being told the ruling would stand. Conwell later became a theologian of note and would help to found Temple University in Philadelphia, Pennsylvania.

Lieutenant Augustus Leazer, after the war, served as Speaker of the House for the North Carolina

General Assembly. While a member of the legislature, he introduced the bill that established an industrial school in Raleigh, later North Carolina State University. He later played an influential role in modernizing the state prisons in North Carolina. Today a North Carolina Historical Marker stands near the site of his home in Rowan County.

Adjutant Josiah Livingston, with Lieutenants Erastus Jewett and Theodore Peck, in 1891 were awarded the United States of America's highest military decoration, the Medal of Honor, for their heroic rear guard actions at the close of the Battle of Newport Barracks.

Brigadier General James Martin led his brigade in the Bermuda Hundred Campaign and at Cold Harbor, before resigning due to his health. Late in the war he commanded the Department of Western North Carolina where he surrendered in 1865. After the war he was an attorney in Asheville, North Carolina where he is buried.

Lieutenant Colonel Valentine Barney went home to his wife Maria, and after the war worked with his father in their marble business. In the 1870's he moved west and lived in Minneapolis and Iowa City where he passed away in 1884, twenty years after the Battle of Newport Barracks.

Private Thomas Dula served as an infantryman and later a drummer in the 42nd North Carolina. After the war Dula went back to his home in Western North Carolina. A few years later he was accused in the murder of Laura Foster and was defended at his trial by Zebulon Vance, the Civil War Governor of North Carolina. Dula, despite Vance's best defense, was found guilty of murder and executed. A ballad would be written about Dula and the crime he was said to have committed. With a bit of artistic liberty Dula gained notoriety as Tom Dooley and the *Ballad of Tom Dooley* was born. It was later a hit song for the Kingston Trio.

In 1946, a year after World War Two ended, a man by the name of George A. Coburn passed away at the age of 101 in Minturn, Colorado. On January 1,

1864, Coburn had enlisted in Company F of the 9th Vermont. One month and a day later took part in the Battle of Newport Barracks. He was the last survivor of the 9th Vermont and quite likely the last surviving veteran of the Battle of Newport Barracks.[16]

---

[16] *Wickman*, XIV

Appendix A:

Roster of Confederate and Union Casualties from February 2, 1864

The following are the names of all known casualties (killed or died of wounds, wounded, or missing/captured) from the fighting on February 2, 1864 in and around Newport Barracks. The roster was compiled from the Service Records of the Confederate and Union units involved in the fighting.

Confederate Killed or Died of Wounds:

5th North Carolina Cavalry

Company E:
First Lieutenant Noah Muse

17th North Carolina Infantry

Company B:
Captain James Leith

Company L:
Sergeant Joseph Elliot

42nd North Carolina Infantry

Company C:
Private James Coley
Private John Poplin Jr.

Company G:
Private William Leazer

Confederate Wounded:

17th North Carolina Infantry

Company C:
Private William Thomas Weathersbee

Company F:
Corporal Cameron Oakley

Company G:
Private James L.G. Davis

Company K:
Private Robert Carney

Company L:
Private Paul Barnheart

Union Killed or Died of Wounds:

9th Vermont Infantry

Company C:
Private Joseph Osier
Private Peter Osier

Company D:
Sergeant William Piper
Private Nathan Smith

Company G:
Private Matthew Riley

Union Wounded:

9th Vermont Infantry

Field and Staff:
Adjutant Josiah Livingston

Company A:
Sergeant Charles Branch
Private Nelson Roberts

Company B:
Private Nathan Deforge
Private George Durkee
Private William Smith

Company C:
Lieutenant James Bolton
Private James Grace
Private Charles Van Steenburg

Company D:
Private Thomas Garry
Private Guy Walker

Company H:
Private Stephen Burrows
Private Thomas Marcy

Company K:
Private Charles Stoddard

Union Captured:

* The asterisk denotes those who died while in captivity in a Confederate prison.

9th Vermont Infantry

Company A:
Private Burchard Clough *
Private Oscar Davis *
Private George Loud *
Private Zara Proud *
Private Harlow Smith *

Company B:
Private Franklin Caswell *
Private Henry Fletcher
Private John Grant
Private Franklin Ives *
Private William Jenks
Private Thomas Ripley *
Private Thomas Rudd
Private David Weller *

Company C:
Private Peter Barton *
Private Henry Beedle *
Private Charles Bennett *
Private James Downer
Private Nelson Stinehowe

Company D:
Private Henry Cobb
Private Philip Duphiney
Private Patrick Manion *
Private George Pearsons *
Private Elbridge Rounsevel *
Private Abel Whitney *

Company F:
Corporal Alson Blake
Private John Clark
Private Alfred Tatro *
Private William Melcher

Company G:
Private Olcott Bacon *
Lieutenant William Holman
Private Lewis Raymore *
Private Milo Tucker *

Company H:
Private Henry Chase
Private Alvin Cole *
Private John Finegan
Private Charles Freeman *
Private Edward Havens *
Private Wayne Hazen *
Private Henry Jackson
Private Patrick McGovern
Private Thomas Pettit *
Private Herman Phelps *
Private Benjamin Smith*
Private Jason Vosburgh

Company I:
Private Franklin Averill *
Private Washington Beede *
Private Joseph Bohonan *
Private Charles George

Company K:
Private Thomas Griswold

<u>23rd New York Cavalry</u>

Company A:
Corporal William Boller *
Corporal Charles Chappell
Corporal Jefferson Moore
Private Walter Ross *

Company B:
Private John Dean *
Private Julius Geschwind
Private Johnnes Leutzinger *
Private Simon Muller
Private Domnic Schneider
Private Conrad Waltz *

2nd Massachusetts Heavy Artillery

Company D:
Private Abel Collins *
Private Michael Flavin *
Private Patrick Fraher *
Private Mark Nalor *
Private William Snow

Appendix B:

Medal of Honor Recipients at the Battle of Newport Barracks, February 2, 1864

On September 8, 1891, three officers who served in the 9th Vermont at the Battle of Newport Barracks on February 2, 1864 were awarded the Medal of Honor.[1] The Medal of Honor is the highest award for valor in action against an enemy force which can be bestowed upon an individual serving in the Armed Services of the United States.

The award is generally presented to its recipient by the President of the United States of America in the name of Congress.[2] The Medal of Honor was established on July 12, 1862, when President Abraham Lincoln signed into law a Joint Resolution of Congress.[3]

The Medal of Honor is awarded to those who whose actions are marked "conspicuously by gallantry

---

[1] *Zeller*, 139

[2] Congressional Medal of Honor Society, *http://www.cmohs.org/*

[3] Ibid. *http://www.cmohs.org/medal-history.php*

and intrepidity at the risk of his life above and beyond the call of duty while engaged in an action against an enemy of the United States." In addition the deed performed must "have been one of personal bravery or self-sacrifice so conspicuous as to clearly distinguish the individual above his comrades and must have involved risk of life.[4]"

Of the 2.5 million men to serve in the United States Army during the American Civil War only 1,522 Medals of Honor were award.[5] Of the 1,522 awarded, three would ultimately be given to men for their actions at Newport Barracks on February 2, 1864.

Adjutant Josiah Livingston, Lieutenant Erastus Jewett, and Lieutenant Theodore Peck all played major roles in the rear guard actions in the final stages of the Battle of Newport Barracks. Their stoic

---

4 United States of America Code of Federal Regulations: Title 32, Volume 2, Part 578, Section 578.4 A, *http://edocket.access.gpo.gov/cfr_2002/julqtr/32cfr578.4.htm*

5 Congressional Medal of Honor Society, *http://www.cmohs.org/medal-statistics.php*

defense and subsequent destruction of the two bridges over the Newport River saved the outnumbered garrison of Newport Barracks from certain capture by Confederate forces of superior number.

Josiah Livingston, former Adjutant of the 9th Vermont and after the war a lawyer in Montpelier, Vermont, wrote a letter to Secretary of War Redfield Proctor on August 20, 1891 in regards to the lack of recognition for two officers he served with in the 9th Vermont Infantry during the war. The two officers mentioned were Lieutenants Erastus Jewett and Theodore Peck for their actions at the Battle at Newport Barracks twenty-seven years earlier.[6] Livingston started his letter as follows:

> It has been on my mind for a long time to write you in regard to the personal bravery and courage of the following officers of the Ninth Vermont Regiment, trusting that is might be your pleasure to have medals of honor which are issued by Congress presented to them.

Livingston later in the letter wrote:

---

[6] *Wickman*, 464

> Lieuts. Jewett and Peck remained at the front long after they were ordered to retreat, and had it not been for their especial gallantry and tenacity, I doubt if we had ever reached the river, as the enemy were well upon our flank and were pushing for the county bridge.[7]

Before the letter was forwarded to Secretary of War Proctor, Livingston sent a copy to the Adjutant General of Vermont Theodore Peck, for his endorsement. The same Theodore Peck, whose actions on February 2, 1864 were one of the reasons for the letter being sent. After reading the letter, Peck brought it to the attention of Erastus Jewett, the other officer mentioned in the letter by Livingston. Both, greatly humbled and touched by the letter, but felt there was one officer whose heroic service that day was absent. That officer was Josiah Livingston. Together they crafted an additional recommendation for a Medal of Honor for Livingston. Jewett and Peck stated that Livingston:

> Does not mention his own personal daring and bravery in the firing of the railroad bridge above mentioned although being wounded in the hand while lighting the match; also his

---

[7] Ibid.

assisting a wounded officers over this bridge when the same was burning. We beg to state that had not Adjutant Livingston remained on the bridge and with his own hands spread the tar and turpentine, we are fearful it would not have been burned, and the story of the engagement above mentioned would have been different.[8]

With the additional nomination, the letter was sent on to Washington to the office of the Secretary of War, now Lewis Grant (the acting Secretary of War) who took over for Proctor after he was appointed to a vacant United States Senate seat by the Governor of Vermont. Both natives of Vermont, Proctor and Grant had served in the Army of the Potomac in the war. On August 29, 1891, Lewis Grant gave the following directive: "Issue medal of honor to Lieutenants Jewett and Peck and Adjutant Livingston for gallantry in action at Newport Barracks, N.C. February 2, 1864.[9]" On September 8, 1891 all three members of the 9th Vermont would be awarded the highest decoration of valor by the United States for their actions at Newport Barracks on February 2, 1864.

---

[8] Wickman, 465

[9] Ibid.

The following are the citations issued with their Medals of Honor:

<u>Lieutenant Erastus W. Jewett:</u>
Company A, 9th Vermont Volunteer Infantry

"By long and persistent resistance and burning the bridges kept a superior force of the enemy at a distance and thus covered the retreat of the garrison.[10]"

<u>Adjutant Josiah O. Livingston:</u>
9th Vermont Volunteer Infantry

"When, after desperate resistance, the small garrison had been driven back to the river by a vastly superior force, this officer, while a small force held back the enemy, personally fired the railroad bridge, and,

---

[10] Recipient Details of Erastus W. Jewett, Congressional Medal of Honor Society, *http://www.cmohs.org/recipient-detail/698/jewett-erastus-w.php*

although wounded himself, assisted a wounded officer over the burning structure.[11]"

Lieutenant Theodore S. Peck:
Company H, 9th Vermont Volunteer Infantry

"By long and persistent resistance and burning the bridges, kept a superior force of the enemy at bay and covered the retreat of the garrison.[12]"

---

[11] Recipient Details of Josiah O. Livingston, Congressional Medal of Honor Society, *http://www.cmohs.org/recipient-detail/807/livingston-josiah-o.php*

[12] Recipient Details of Theodore S. Peck, Congressional Medal of Honor Society, *http://www.cmohs.org/recipient-detail/1046/peck-theodore-s.php*

Ten Roads Publishing, LLC

For more information on this title or to schedule a speaking engagement or media appearance by the author please call 252-725-0451, or you can contact us via email at:

info@tenroadspublishing.com

or visit our website at:

www.tenroadspublishing.com

About the Author

Eric A. Lindblade was born and raised in North Carolina, and began his study of the Civil War after his first trip to Gettysburg at the age of six. He attended East Carolina University and is the co-owner of Ten Roads Publishing, LLC. He currently lives in Gettysburg, Pennsylvania. *Fight As Long As Possible: The Battle of Newport Barracks, North Carolina, February 2, 1864* is his first book. He is currently working on a comprehensive roster of North Carolina soldiers who were casualties during the Battle of Gettysburg, with a follow up volume covering the 1862 Maryland Campaign. He also maintains a blog focusing on the Battle of Newport Barracks and Newport, North Carolina during the Civil War at http://newportbarracks.blogspot.com/.

www.ingramcontent.com/pod-product-compliance
Lightning Source LLC
LaVergne TN
LVHW051347080426
835509LV00020BA/3317